PARISH

COUNSELING

COMMENTARY

The pastor has an unusual opportunity to counsel those people who would not ordinarily make an appointment with a psychiatrist. He can help them, often without their knowing that they are in a counseling process. In this book Dr. Jackson describes how the pastor can apply the special skills of the counselor to major life events, problems, and needs of his congregation, showing the psychological processes and types of therapeutic interventions the pastor may employ and illustrating these with examples from his own counseling experience.

Dr. Jackson has brought to the ministry an interest and background in the mental health professions that spans forty years. His book shows the pastor how to continue his education in the helping professions, and provides a valuable resource for the pastor who may not be able to afford the time to go back to school in order to keep up with the rapid advances in pastoral care and counseling that have taken place over the last few years. The case studies in *Parish Counseling* reveal such counseling to be the most valid base for the ministry, giving the pastor an opportunity to meet people where they live, to observe the impact of environment on their lives, and to discover those strengths that can be built on therapeutically.

PARISH COUNSELING

by

Edgar N. Jackson, D.D.

New York • Jason Aronson • London

to

Seward Hiltner

a pioneer in disciplined pastoral counseling

Foreword

Why I Wrote *Parish Counseling*

When in my first parish assignment forty years ago I found myself as a chaplain for twenty-eight hundred mentally disturbed patients, I also quickly found that nothing I had learned in seminary was relevant to the task I faced. So after two years of frustrating activity I went back to school for five years to try to discover the resources for ministering to people with special needs.

Soon I came upon some wise counsel that had to do with the pastor's counseling role in the more carefully structured setting of campus, hospital and counseling room. But it seemed to me that the pastor encountered his people in settings that did not permit careful structuring, but that demanded far more skill and imagination than the insulated setting of the counseling room.

For years I sought to develop a modality that met the unique setting of the parish and at the same time made use of the special skills and insights that were so much a part of the counselor's training.

The pastor in the parish meets people in a wide variety of activities. He can always be observing, listening and in many ways preparing himself for the time when people with their special needs will seek him. Also in his normal parish activities he shares important life events and is able to be alert to problems, needs and possibilities for wise intervention.

I believe that the pastor in the parish has an unusual opportunity to counsel people who would not make an appointment with a counselor. He can counsel them often without their knowing that they are in fact in a counseling process.

In this book I have tried briefly to outline my concept of parish counseling as a unique modality with its own limitations and opportunities. I have tried to indicate how a parish counseling ministry can be developed and how the pastor can carry on a continuing process of his own education.

But I have tried to make the parish counseling process speak for itself. In eighteen encounters drawn from my own experience but carefully disguised to protect the confidence implicit in all counseling, I have tried to show something of the process, the types of psychological movement and therapeutic intervention that is possible.

Certainly this is not offered as any final word on the counseling role in the parish. Rather it is an effort to stimulate discussion and exploration of an important aspect of the counseling ministry that has often been neglected in the past because of limitation implicit in the training centers or because those with the special skill did not appreciate the special opportunities that the parish affords for counseling.

Perhaps this book will help to sharpen up those needed skills that can help the pastor work with that large group of people who are where they are, in the parish.

EDGAR N. JACKSON

Contents

INTRODUCTION

The basic concerns of parish counseling are both old and new. Since the caretaking profession first defined its interests there has been a desire to minister to the needs of those who suffered in body, mind and spirit. The priest and the prophet shared an active interest in what happened to people. The healing arts were often entrusted to the care of the priestly cult. The saint was marked by his self-giving concern for others, and St. Francis walked among his fellowmen with a desire and a skill to heal the broken hearts, the diseased bodies and the disturbed minds of his day.

A new modality has emerged to give direction and substance to the ancient concern. The inevitable amalgamation of the pastoral interest in people's welfare and the new skills of the mental health movement combine in something that is so new that it has not been fully recognized for what it is, a major new development in the health care field.

This new modality is centered at the point where the professional person lives in most intimate contact with the largest number of people with acute needs. It is the pastor at work in his parish. It is the potentially skilled counselor working in a unique setting to perform both a major preventive activity and a significant form of therapeutic intervention.

Let us spell out the nature of this new dimension of the pastoral function in the living parish. In the chapters that follow we will be elaborating the processes of pastoral care through parish counseling and illustrating it by a number of parish encounters between the pastor and his people. But before we do that we need to sharpen what it is we will be examining and why we feel that it is a unique process.

Often the most important things going on around us are ignored simply because they are so close to us, so much a part of our existence, that we take them for granted. The history of social change is replete with the illustrations of major changes that have taken place so gradually that they have been ignored. The polluting of the atmosphere was going on gradually for decades before anyone became concerned enough to make an issue of it. Major population shifts were taking place gradually before we began to be aware of the impact of these forms of group uprooting with their changes in attitudes and values.

So, too, with the emerging of parish counseling as a unique and valued tool for anticipating personality crises and contributing to their wise resolution. Many pastors knew they were at the center of emotional crises. They sensed the impact of these crises on the lives of the people they served. They dimly envisioned the significance of their pastoral role in serving these people. But because the professional and cultural changes came on so gradually, they often were content to try to meet new opportunities with old tools or were so threatened by the responsibilities that they turned their backs on the privileged moments of pastoral circumstance that afforded them times to act out their human concern.

Sometimes it is a matter of waiting for the development of a new science or a new mode of thought. For instance, there was little interest in the problems of the grieving until my book *Un-*

derstanding Grief was published in 1957. The unique role of the pastor at work in the parish was seen more clearly for what it really was after my book on crisis psychology and crisis management brought into sharper focus the growing body of research on the significance of crises and the importance of their wise management.

Now it seems clear that we can see what has been happening and what the meaning of it is for the pastor who serves his people in the parish context. This pastor who lives close to his people and observes their lives in a variety of different roles may be the person who can provide the most valid form of therapeutic intervention in the vortex of changing life styles and social adjustment.

But the pastor at work in the parish can do this important work best, it seems, when he puts together four modalities that converge at the point where he works and through the concern that he represents. It is at this point of conscious concern and circumstantial convergence that he will sense his purpose, develop his new skills, achieve a more significant ministry and become a fulfilled and unthreatened individual in his role with the people he serves.

Let us look at the four modalities. First, there is the theological base the pastor employs. Second is the tradition of pastoral care and concern and the personal and institutional history that undergirds the concern. Third is the achievement of professional skills that grows from a knowledge of the literature and an implementing of the insights of the contemporary mental health movement. And fourth is the fusion of these resources at the point where the pastor functions, in the unique social institution called the parish.

While we will be looking at some of these points in more detail later, let us look at them in as sharp and precise a form as possible now so that we will understand where we are going and why.

When we speak of a theological base we are not speaking in terms of the narrow confines of concepts over which denominational disputes arise. Rather, we are speaking of the broad base of ideas that motivate a man and determine the bounds of his pastoral concern. These ideas have to do with the nature of man, his cosmic value and the methods that can be employed to bring him to the highest level of personal functioning. It relates to what a man is and what he can become.

Secular modalities may have an implicit theological base, but it does not usually become explicit. The pastor not only has the resource of a theological base from which he operates but he can make it explicit as part of what he works with in evaluating a man and giving worth to his self-concept as he struggles to cope with life in its most worthy terms.

The Biblical base for these theological concepts is active and practical rather than theoretical and abstract. Job is dealing with real suffering, and Jesus is speaking to and touching real people. The early church was a living body of shared concern and helpfulness. It reached to all of the personal and social dimensions of life.

The pastor cannot separate himself from that tradition even if he tries, for people keep investing him with the history and tradition. Rather than try to escape from the inescapable, the pastor may use this unique tradition as a significant resource in his work with people.

The pastor is never just himself. He is a person who stands for something. He is a man who believes in a redemptive power at work to help people overcome the destructive circumstances of life and find new wholeness. He is not ashamed of this tradition, but rather values it as a representation of theology in action. He does not have to deny or gloss over the failure of the institution to use its positive attitudes toward man and his problems.

The implicit pastoral, shepherding concern is a unique resource in parish counseling as it moves people toward their pastor and the pastor toward his people. In no other professional relationship is this fundamental relationship so clearly spelled out. It would be tragic if this resource were ignored. It is a base for wise and useful human relationships and counseling possibilities when it is clearly recognized and wisely used.

Second, the pastor needs to appreciate fully the part that the institution plays in his work with people. It provides the point of contact with people of all ages and in all conditions. It is a center for education, for inspiration, for common concerns and social relatedness. Within this context the pastor can be the friend, the priest, the teacher, the spiritual guide and the social worker. He has more points of contact whereby he can relate to the people he serves than any other professional person. If he is alert, wise and perceptive this can be a unique resource in his approach to parish counseling.

In our day of rapid movement, with one out of every four families moving every year and millions of single people in constant mobility, a stable institution becomes doubly valuable. Certain characteristics of the church as an institution tend to remain constant, and desirably so. The church is a meeting place for people who seek meaning for life. It is centered about processes of establishing worth for life, its worshiping function. It is concerned with providing ceremonial resources for acting out deep feelings. It seeks to provide spiritual guidance for those lost and confused. It is dedicated to personal discovery and growth. It provides communal resources for achieving these varied purposes.

The religious institution is a unique center for seeking personal goals because it is the only organization that exists solely to aid in personal and spiritual growth. However devious its activity may at times seem, its only purpose is ultimately to help people become more valid and fulfilled individuals.

Third, and this may be the most important of all, is the growth in the understanding of the human personality and its dynamics that directly affect the practice of pastoral care.

It may well be that at no previous time in history has the modality for pastoral care gone through such rapid and basic changes. The only parallel might be the impact on medical practice of the discovery of the germ theory and the development of antibiotics.

No pastor can now serve his people with a clear conscience unless he makes a strenuous effort to know what has been discovered about people's inner motivation, how it manifests itself in behavior, what the behavior means and what can be done to wisely guide people from maladaptive and self-destructive behavior toward mental and spiritual health.

Yet the placing of these additional demands on the time and

energy of a pastor may be resisted. He may try to escape his responsibility like the characters in the story of the Good Samari-
tan by employing legalisms, priestly preoccupations and triviali-
ties. But none of these are good enough when confronted by the
person whose needs are great. The pastor is obliged to be the
best-equipped professional he can be.

Yet he also finds it difficult to go back to the setting of formal
education, for schools take time and money. Perhaps the best
resource he can find for his continued growth in competently
working with people would be to set aside two or three hours a
day to read, study, listen to tapes and stimulate himself in the
clinical material, case studies or records of pastoral encounters
that make him sensitive to what is happening to people in the
crises of their lives.

But until he grasps the fact that the unique modality of counseling in the parish is just being born into a new and challenging
specialization, he may let the most valid base for his pastoral
ministry slip through his fingers. As in medical practice, the
trend toward specialization is being re-examined, and the interest in a new approach to medical practice in the specialty of the
general practitioner, the importance of meeting people where
they live, observing the impact of the environment on their lives,
and discovering the strengths in the context of their living that
can be built on therapeutically, the pastor's unique role with
people in the parish opens the way toward a more important and
fruitful ministry.

This leads to the fourth modality that must be emphasized in
understanding the new and challenging approach to the work of
the pastor in the parish. In order to understand what is happening to people it is important to know as much as possible about
people. The specialist may see a person in the hospital, a specialized environment. The physician may see a person in his office, again a specialized environment. Of all members of the
caretaking professions, only the pastor in the parish is privileged
to observe people in the multiple roles of their lives that can best
reveal the meaning of their behavior, psychologically, socially
and organically. He sees them as priest, counselor, educator,
spiritual guide and friend. He has access to their lives at more

points than any other member of the professional community. He has more chance to understand and assess their behavior and what it means than any other member of the therapeutic teams.

The new recognition of the importance of this many-faceted approach to people and their behavior does at least three things for the parish pastor. It clarifies his role as the practitioner of a new treatment modality. It gives new significance to his function in the professional community. And it places new and important responsibilities on him to be worthy of the special opportunity that comes with his pastoral role.

Too often the pastor has had to struggle to find a satisfying identity. Too often he has felt threatened in his relationship to other members of the healing team. Too often he has felt under-equipped for the tasks he sees in his work with people. Now it may well be that he can feel a new sense of the importance of his function and his role in the lives of the people he serves. Now he can with justification stand up as a member of the healing team with a valid function that is clearly recognized by his colleagues. And now he can find the tools that he needs to nurture constantly the growing edge of his professional skill so that he becomes sure of himself as he becomes more competent in his understanding of people and their growth toward true wholeness of body, mind and spirit.

In our dehumanizing culture men need to find a new sense of their humanity. In our culture of life-fracturing specializations men need to be seen as total functioning beings. In our uncertain stance as pastors we need to see the validity and importance of the function of the parish minister who walks the common road with his people. Perhaps more significantly now than ever before in history, the pastor in the parish represents the source of human values, human resources and responsiveness to human needs.

How do we awaken the full realization of this important role in the life of the culture, the church and its people? Perhaps it is a simpler process than we imagine. It may be that it starts with you. It may be that it builds on your growing appreciation of your privileged role. It may be that it is fulfilled in a new aware-

ness of the importance of your dedication to being the best possible pastor you can be wherever you are among the people you
serve. In this mediating of the healing, redeeming love of God,
the Holy Spirit may come alive in and through you.

SECTION ONE: The Roots of Pastoral Involvement and Concern

Chapter 1

Parish Counseling

During the last few decades there has been a development of skills in pastoral counseling. Almost always in the past the philosophy, the techniques and the major areas of practice were developed in institutional settings.

Then came Pope John with his declaration that "the people are the church," and in many ways there has been a subtle but constant shift in emphasis away from institutions to people as they are encountered in the parish.

What Pope John did for the Roman Catholic tradition has been acted on by persons in other religious bodies with a new concern for people as they are found in the major context of their living, in the family, the church, the school and the community.

That means that there is need for a re-examination of the ways in which pastoral care through counseling should be practiced. In these pages we will try to do that.

But in order to look ahead it is essential that we look back a bit and see just what has been happening to bring pastoral care through counseling to the state where it now is.

Pastoral care has been bound up with developments in the research and practice of psychology. Any consideration of pastoral care as the function of the religious counselor working with the emotional problems of his parishioners must begin with recognition of the wide variation of practices that makes any generalization unwise and misleading.

The Roman Catholic tradition has depended largely upon ritualized practices, such as confession, to meet the emotional needs of its people. This tended to meet generalized rather than specific needs of people. In the last couple of decades priests and nuns who are also psychiatrists have begun to change the care of people toward the specific needs of the individual. The teaching of men like Fr. Edward Cassem, M.D., a Jesuit psychiatrist, has had its influence on a new generation of parish priests. Well-written and psychologically sound textbooks written by Catholic psychiatrists are now used in the education of parish priests.

The Jewish tradition, with its scholarly preoccupations, has been aware of both the importance of ancient traditions and folkways and also the insights of contemporary science and research. Jewish persons have made major contributions to psychological insight in the last seventy-five years. Rabbi Earl Grollman's study of Freud and Rabbinical counseling has focused attention on the philosophical assumptions of wise counseling. It is interesting to note how much of the basic philosophy of the nature of man has permeated this psychological contribution. Even when the philosophical premises wore thin, the tendency has been to revert to a way of looking at man that could counteract the predominantly pessimistic emphasis of mechanistic psychological systems.

Perhaps the major interest in pastoral psychology and its application in parish counseling emerged from the Protestant tradition. This is only natural, because the need for pastoral care on an individualized basis was one of the conditions that led to the Protestant Reformation. Also the exploration of pastoral psychology gave another opportunity to Protestant ministers to continue their endless and elusive quest for an identity. This we will explore more at length in a later chapter.

Today in the United States more than twenty thousand pastors have had specialized training in pastoral care. This does not refer merely to college or seminary courses in the psychology of religion and personality, but means specifically that they have had courses involving an intensive clinical experience under supervision, usually in a general or psychiatric hospital, of from three months' to three years' duration. This means that a fairly large body of pastors have had psychiatrically supervised study as well as practical experience with reasonably sophisticated psychological assumptions. While it is still only about 10 per cent of the pastors in service, it certainly is a numerically larger group than any other profession with psychological training available to people in local communities.

This increased interest in understanding people and their mental and emotional problems has developed for at least three basic reasons.

One has been the increased interest on the part of the general public in the meaning of emotional stress and its related behavior. Psychosomatic research has related emotional states to a wide variety of physical and social behavior. This has led to awareness of need that brings hundreds of thousands of persons every year to their pastors for counsel and guidance. Columnists and others urge people to talk over their problems with a counselor. The pastor is most accessible. In fact the Joint Commission on Mental Health has documented this by pointing out that 42 per cent of people with problems go first to their pastors, as compared with 29 per cent who seek out a physician.

A second reason that is closely related to the first is the feeling many pastors have had that they were inadequately prepared by their seminary education to meet this expanded interest in and need for pastoral counseling by their parishioners. So they have tried to improve their skills and competence in response to these needs. And like any good thing, without any effort to advertise their interest or training, those who benefited from this new form of pastoral service told others and the nature of the pastoral ministry began to change markedly because of the demand

and the increased supply of competent parish counselors.

In large areas of the country where few psychologists or psychiatrists are available, if parishioners were to have professional counseling at all it would be to their religious counselor that they would be obliged to turn.

From these two reasons has emerged a third that may become increasingly important in years ahead. With the general breakdown of theological systems the trained professional within the religious community has sought new ways to make his life and ministry significant. He could no longer be either intellectually or emotionally comfortable with the old cosmology or the old psychology and was casting about, as it were, for a new religious role. Pastoral psychology both in theory and in practice gave the pastor a new validity of being and new and significant forms of ministry at the same time that it made the old ways of looking at man and the universe historically understandable even if not currently relevant.

This change in pastoral role and attitude has led to a new body of literature and professional standards for pastoral work. A new awareness of the emotional and social meaning of old ways of doing things has brought into focus a new interest in and need for the appreciation of rites, rituals and ceremonials. The language of symbolism with its broad basis for emotional meaning has been stated with new relevance by Rollo May, Ira Progoff and Jergen Ruesch. At the same time the need for an adequate concept of the nature of man as a basis for comprehending his behavior has led to a re-examination of the wonder and mystery of consciousness in all of its breadth and depth. This has given a new relevance to the basic assumptions about the spiritual nature of man and his experience.

Seward Hiltner, Carroll Wise and Wayne Oates have worked hard to set up adequate standards of training and practice for those who engage in pastoral counseling, and national organizations to supervise these standards have been set up across the country. This effort has stimulated a more truly professional awareness among those who work with people psychologically and spiritually.

Too often the theological seminaries have been slow to recognize the importance of pastoral care. Traditional studies like theology, church history and Biblical studies with their inherited status have been slow to recognize the importance of basic concern with people. It is also easier to cope with abstract ideas than concrete people, both theoretically and in practice. However, changes are taking place even in conservative settings, and the body of literature, the professional journals and the professional organizations are making their impact felt.

While a slow start has been made in seminaries, a major effort has been engaged in through seminars, clinical training programs, graduate study in secular settings and independent action by pastors who seek to improve their knowledge and skills in pastoral care.

This independent action has guaranteed a freedom of exploration that has stimulated communication of an interdisciplinary and interprofessional nature, and the libraries of pastors are now bulging with books by anthropologists, psychologists, psychiatrists, sociologists and authors in other areas of specialization in the study and understanding of man, that newly viewed and amazingly interesting creature.

The development of pastoral psychology has helped the pastor to discover a new sense of personal and social freedom. He can respect his basic function with people as well as his essential view of man as a person who can be helped to newness of life. Even the rigidity of the religious institutions seems to be changing under the impact of this concern with people as they are. So the archaic institutional structure may be changed by new life from within before they collapse from their burdensome superstructure.

The rediscovery of the parish as the center of life and valid therapeutic endeavor may have wider ramifications than have been heretofore recognized. Not only may it give new status and satisfaction to the parish pastor in doing his important work with people, but it may well also serve as a way of revitalizing the church as a resource for discovering meaning in the midst of so much else in life that appears to be meaningless.

It may well be important for us, then, to spend some time exploring this important activity of parish counseling, to try to understand its possibilities and its limitations, its origins and its directions, its hazards and its rewards. To that end we direct our efforts.

Chapter 2

The Literature

Pastors are men of the Book and the books. What is written becomes important to them. Too often they are isolated members of a community who have no one with whom they can share their thoughts and feelings. So books become people, and ideas become companions. But books not only fracture the lonely isolation, they may well become the molders of life and practice.

Perhaps the nature of the change in parish work and the influences that stimulate it can be best shown by noting those who are now quoted, studied and followed as guides in the understanding of man and his nature. The pastor is interested in finding a psychological system that is valid for our day. Yet he quite naturally seeks a philosophical base that does not violate his traditional way of looking at life. If he can follow a psychologist who recognizes the importance of religious motivation, symbolic formulations and ritualized practice as well as parish counseling he will be more apt to accept that leadership than that of a psychologist who categorically rejects religion and equates it with forms of mental illness and emotional disturbance. It is interesting then to look at the thinkers to whom status has been accorded as the theoretical leaders of the pastoral psychology movement of our day.

Anton Boisen is considered by many to be the pioneer spirit in opening up the religious study of the disturbed person. He looked in upon himself and found much to share with his colleagues who tried to understand the mentally ill. His book *The Exploration of the Inner World* has been a landmark in pastoral care study.

Russell Dicks, with a physician, Richard Cabot, wrote *The Art of Ministering to the Sick*, which gave new depth to the role the pastor had traditionally had with the ill. It enriched pastoral communication so that what the pastor said and did was not only a source of comfort but might also have therapeutic significance in the teamwork that could develop in the hospital and the home.

Seward Hiltner, through his important book *Pastoral Counseling*, set the standard for a whole generation of effort to refine and upgrade the professional work of the pastor. Other significant works gave standing to the pastor as a counselor whose integrity and obligation were comparable to those of other members of the therapeutic team.

The present writer helped to bring into focus the role of the pastor in crisis management with his books *Understanding Grief* and *Coping with the Crises in Your Life*. Because most people come to the pastor when a crisis develops, this important role cannot only provide opportunity for wise counseling but also enrich on a permanent basis the pastor-parishioner relationship.

However, the influence of several popularizers of psychological insight has influenced parish counselors quite as much as have their colleagues just mentioned.

Clifford Beers brought the mysteries of mental illness and therapeutic intervention out of the textbooks and into life with his autogiobraphy *The Mind That Found Itself*. Out of his own experience and the need for friendly understanding he started the American Foundation for Mental Hygiene. Many pastors first became acquainted with the problems of the mentally disturbed through that organization and its successor, the Mental Health Association.

Rollo May, a pastor turned psychoanalyst and teacher, also gave a new relevance to the teachings of the psychologists. His book *The Art of Counseling* was a new experience for pastors who read it. It made the process less remote and more understandable. His later books, *The Meaning of Anxiety*, *Man's Search for Himself* and *Love and Will*, helped many pastors to become familiar with the material of therapeutic intervention.

Fritz Kunkel, a psychotherapist, implied that Jesus was an expert psychologist and that his followers should find no mystery in the psychological process. His book *In Search of Maturity* gave the impression that the pastor's role was to help people grow up into true spiritual maturity as a solution of many of life's problems. This was an idea most pastors could feel comfortable with, and this book was the basis for much pastoral counseling for years.

Paul Tournier, a European psychiatrist, made case material come alive in the context of Biblical quotations and ideas. Many pastors felt comfortable with his thoughts and read his books not only for verification of their Biblically oriented approach but as well for their own guidance and security. His books *The Meaning of Persons* and *A Doctor's Casebook in the Light of the Bible* were perhaps most influential.

The main function of these popularizers was to open the door for a more careful study of a dozen innovators who were not always religiously oriented but whose insight had value for pastoral work. These are not mentioned in order of importance or chronologically, for all were of necessity contemporaneous.

Erich Fromm used the opportunity of the Yale Lectures to stimulate a whole new awareness of the relation of religion to psychoanalysis. His studies such as *The Dogma of Christ* and *Man for Himself* have focused thought on mood and manner that needed to be examined in a clear, candid light. Also his sympathetic understanding of the spiritual meaning of Zen has given to his work a hospitality toward the religious impulse that made it illuminating without suggesting any hostility.

Paul Tillich, though a theologian, approached man and his existential problem with a concern for the basic nature of being. His concept of religion warranted a search for the emotional drive of life or the courage to be what man could be. Paul Hoch in his symposium used Tillich's interpretation of anxiety as a fresh starting point for a wholly new look at the meaning of anxiety and the understanding of its existential roots as a premise for therapeutic intervention.

Carl Rogers with his rather optimistic view of human nature has had a strong influence on pastoral psychology. His system for releasing the inner resources of the person has had wide acceptance among pastors and teachers of parish counseling. His newly developed interest in group processes further employs the pastor's multiple roles with people. When it is possible to create the clearly clinical atmosphere, which is so often the case in the parish, Rogers' philosophy and methods seem compatible with the pastor's environment for working with people. When a pastor was not quite sure of his skills, he could feel comfortable with the educative technique. Probably more pastors in parishes have used modifications of the Rogerian technique than any other one form of counseling. The implicit theological concepts of Rogers have also made the parish counselor feel more comfortable with the method.

Harry Stack Sullivan in his unique interpretation of symbolic structures of thought and language, as well as the strong place he makes for interpersonal relationships in any therapeutic process, has given warrant for parish counselors to see new meanings in organizational work and parish programs that had been inadequately appreciated before. The variety of opportunities the religious organizations make available for people to be together and talk out their emotional concerns become quite a different thing when assayed from the point of view of Sullivan's basic philosophy.

Perhaps the champion, at least during the earlier periods of development, for most parish counselors, especially in Roman Catholic ranks, has been Carl Jung. Though a son of a Protes-

tant pastor, Jung made studies of the complicated rites and ceremonies of the Roman Catholic church, which, through their
objectivity, made it possible for those who practiced the rites to
find new and important meanings there that had long escaped
them. And while many pastors did not understand the rather
complicated conceptual structure of his system, they felt it must
be acceptable, for his break with Freud tended to make him a
psychological hero even to overlooking his painfully inept
adjustment to Hitler's racial and social concepts.

Because religion's primary concern has always been an answer to the question "Why?"—the basic question of meaning—
the logotherapy of Viktor Frankl has stimulated wide interest
and considerable acceptance among pastoral counselors. His
emphasis on the quest for life's meaning as essential to the therapeutic process is akin to the most exalted function of the spiritual guide of religious tradition. The relevance of his own personal experience in seeking spiritual resources adequate for
life's most harrowing experiences gives some of the elements of
inspiration that have always been important to the spiritually
oriented individual. His books *The Doctor and the Soul, The
Will to Meaning* and *From Prison Camp to Existentialism* have
been widely read by pastors and have deeply influenced their
feelings about the counseling process.

Interestingly enough, Freud, who was once considered a
threat to the interpreter of religious meaning, has in recent years
come into new recognition among pastors. This is partly due to
the humanizing impact of writings by Ernest Jones and Irving
Stone, as well as the interpretation given his work by Earl Grollman in *Freud and Rabbinical Counseling*. Also it may be due to
the fact that Freud has been read increasingly in the original,
and this has brought the real Freud into new acceptance with
pastors who have sensed his deep human concerns. Also the significance of the spoken word as an instrument of healing has
come into new prominence through Freud. As speech is the basic tool of the pastor, Freud became his champion. Then, too,
the more objective view of Freud made it possible to look beyond
his rather limited scientific orientation to the great clinical insights he achieved into the nature of man and his behavior. And

with time even a grudging recognition of his major theoretical contributions was enough to overcome the misunderstanding that underlay the earlier apprehension and hostility.

Some of the remaining instability among pastoral counselors, however, is reflected in the rather wide, enthusiastic and uncritical acceptance of the ideas and writings of O. Hobart Mowrer. His restoration of sin as a fact of life and his emphasis on moral responsibility as basic to mental health seemed a valid basis for restoring to some pastors their main emotional weapon, an appeal to neurotic guilt. This seems to give clear evidence that for many, at least, the unexamined premises of the past are not easily dislodged by the newer insights of the present. It is fortunate that a more seasoned and objective view has been brought back into thought on this subject by Karl Menninger's book *What Ever Became of Sin?*

Jurgen Ruesch with his four books on communication has spoken rather directly to the pastor who has traditionally found his influence through his ability as a communicator. He has helped many pastors to understand their own motivations in speaking at the same time that he has helped them develop a new sensitivity to the efforts of others to externalize their emotional pressure points. His practical insight into the processes of disturbed and therapeutic communication has been especially useful to the pastor's role as a perceptive listener and responsive guide.

Otto Rank with his soul theory and his emphasis on early influences in personality development has struck two chords that invite a sympathetic response from pastors. Both concepts have tended to place the human being back in the mainstream of thought about man as a creature of special endowment and circumstantial response rather than merely a complicated chemical factory, responding with never erring predictability to a variety of external stimuli. His work has stimulated those especially interested in religious development of personality to understand the importance of group work with parents so that the earliest influences can be directed toward the emotional security of the child.

At the theoretical level one cannot overlook the impact of the thinking of Martin Buber. His contribution to the underlying philosophy of modern psychology has been more important than this generation will easily recognize. The formulation of the meaning of human, social and cosmic relations has been so sharp and relevant that it has reached into every avenue of human consideration. No psychological formulations acceptable to the religious thinker would be apt to ignore Buber's thought.

Abraham Maslow with his studies of the psychologically healthy and creative individual has added an ingredient that the proponents of modern pastoral care have welcomed. His definition of the profile of the self-actualizing, self-fulfilling person lends itself to the goals that the worker within the parish seeks. The pastoral ministry is different from the usual clinical or institutional program because it works with people who would generally be considered closer to the normal and healthy than to the abnormal and diseased. His is a welcome source of insight just because it focuses on those who are not viewed as morbid personalities or unhealthy case material.

Though the contributions of these innovators vary considerably in theological, philosophical and psychological presuppositions, they make a base from which the developers of the modern pastoral psychology movement can draw the material they need for creating something that employs what they consider the best of the old as well as the best of the new.

Supplementing these individual thinkers are three generalized areas of special interest: sex, health and institutions. Each of these areas has built up its own authorities, writers and researchers as well as its programs for promoting its insights within pastoral psychology.

Sex and religion have always been interrelated, though in more recent times the emphasis has been on control, restraint or denial of sex by religious groups. This has been reflected in sacred writings, in the context of myth and legend, in such doctrinal concepts as asexual birth, and the practice of celibacy. Such emphases tend to make it difficult to be realized, because on one side there is over-restraint and on the other over-indulgence. These attitudes often become projected into counseling on sexual or family matters.

Freud's examination of sex as a motivating force in life has led to a re-examination of attitudes and practices that had been largely unquestioned within religious groups, for it was assumed that they possessed unquestioned truth from revealed sources. Within religious institutions a new understanding of the importance of healthful sex life has led to changed attitudes toward family-planning, premarital and marriage counseling. Much pastoral counseling now develops around sex and marriage, and the privileged role the pastor has in premarital education and the ceremonial events attendant upon marriage gives him an approachability that is often a useful resource.

The changed modes of life, the alternatives to traditional marriage and new attitudes toward sex often come into the pastor's counseling interest, especially as he is often the mediator between the generations as they seek to cope with new patterns of sexual behavior. Many of the human stress points tend to develop as women seek to find some of the rights increasingly asserted by women's liberation proponents. The new openness and honesty about human sexuality has developed so rapidly that the pastor in the parish needs special help in understanding and interpreting the problems that develop from generation to generation.

A large and articulate group of writers have exerted both a subtle and indirect influence on the pastor as well as a direct and explicit influence on his work with people and their sex problems. This is especially true with problems of homosexual interpretation and the life styles that circumvent traditional modes of sexual behavior.

In the last two or three decades a large number of writers have worked to influence pastoral attitudes toward sex. Too numerous to explore in detail, we can merely mention their names. They are Abraham and Hannah Stone, the Duvalls, the Overstreets, A. C. Kinsey, Masters and Johnson, Walter R. Stokes, Pitirim Sorokin, Emily Mudd, Eustace Chesser, Frank Caprio and David Mace.

Also organizations like the Planned Parenthood Federation and Family Life Conferences have had their impact on practical approaches to pastoral care. Probably the main use by pastors of projective testing devices has developed in premarital counseling, though the results have been used more for opening up discussion than for diagnosis or therapy.

From the time of the jurisdictional disputes of the Greek patrons of health, Asclepius and Hygeia, there has been an active relationship between religion and health or wholeness of being. This has moved through stages of the magical and the miraculous to the more modern understanding of psychosomatic and psychogenic influences on health. Interestingly, the insights of the psychosomaticist put much of the responsibility for the preservation and restoration of health back in the areas of the psychological and the spiritual. Even Jerome Frank's efforts to define the faith factor in medical practice, *Persuasion and Healing*, puts the findings within the realm of the implicitly religious even if it is not made explicitly so.

Perhaps the point at which psychological insight seems to have most influence for the pastoral counselor is at the point of relationship of right thinking and right feeling with the organic behavior we call disease. Flanders Dunbar worked out a degree in Union Theological Seminary before writing *Emotions and Bodily Changes*. Frank Alexander has brought a penetrating insight into historical influences in his study of psychosomatic processes and Grinker and Speigel have used the emotional stresses compounded by wartime conditions to show the impact of feelings on organic function.

The School of Psychiatry and the School of Public Health Medicine at Harvard University have done much to make explicit the nature of a psychology of crisis that fits the needs of a parish counselor as he works with his people at the points where crises touch their lives. Here Lindemann, Erikson, Caplan, Hackett and Wiseman have combined to produce rich material concerning the theoretical insights relevant for therapeutic intervention.

So the research on both sex and health has given valued insights to the pastor who works with people in the context of parish living. The rich literature on these and other subjects mentioned has probably been the major source of education for a whole generation of clergymen and teachers of pastoral care.

While little research has been done in parish life, much of the research of others working in the personality sciences has been adapted and used fruitfully by the thousands of pastors who work actively with their people in confronting life and its problems.

Chapter 3

Institutional Impact

Because some institutions were less bound by tradition they provided the conditions wherein pastoral care practices might be developed more rapidly than in the parish setting. This contribution of institutions cannot be ignored in trying to understand the development of parish counseling. In addition to research in sexual behavior and psychosomatic medicine we must explore the impact of institutional practice on pastoral care and, because so much has been done, must set aside a chapter for that purpose.

Chaplaincies in institutions provide a limited and clearly defined relationship. They give persons with special skills an opportunity to function under conditions that are protected from the multiple intrusions and varied conditions of parish life. Many persons with these special skills have found the institution an advantageous place for exercising their skills. When they

function within the limitations of the institution they are protected by the authority of the institution.

In our country the chaplaincy with the longest history and
largest impact has been within the military establishment. Here,
with a separate, semi-complete and well-regulated community,
the function of the religious counselor has been clearly defined
and more highly specialized than the pastoral function in the
parish. It has been a specialized parish. Most chaplains have
had the benefit of special training in psychology and counseling.
Much of their time has been devoted to counseling sessions with
persons who have a need to talk out the problems of their adjustment to the special community the military represents. This
includes all aspects of military service. Adjustment, hospital,
combat and base assignments for the chaplain's corps are so
dispersed as to make a chaplain-counselor accessible to all personnel.

During World War II thousands of chaplains and millions of
citizens were engaged in this relationship. It proved its value to
chaplains as well as to personnel, and when the war was over
many men wanted to continue a form of ministry that had some
of the benefits of the specialized authority and limited responsibility that the chaplaincy provided.

Since the war, specialized pastoral work has been increased in
hospitals. Many large hospitals have specially trained full-time
chaplains on their staffs. The training usually calls for a year or
more of supervised, psychiatrically oriented work. While only
about a third of the population has active religious affiliations,
nearly everyone who enters a hospital has apprehension, anxiety
and a mood of bafflement at much of hospital routine. The increase of specialization in medical practice tends to depersonalize the treatment of patients. It becomes increasingly important
for there to be someone on the staff who has the time to answer
questions sympathetically and allow the patient to talk about his
thoughts and feelings. The hospital chaplain, as a pastoral psychologist with specialized training, well meets this need, and
while his ministry is usually interdenominational in nature it
cannot help but be religiously important just because he is who
he is and where he is.

Another form of specialized pastoral psychology is practiced by the prison chaplain. "I was in prison and ye came unto me" provides a scriptural basis for this work. Originally this work was usually done on a part-time basis by volunteers in response to a feeling of social responsibility to condemned men. The appointment of full-time chaplains to penal institutions has been but another part of the move toward more enlightened and humane treatment of social offenders. Here the special skills of the religious counselor combine the insight of sociology and psychology in the understanding of the cause-effect relationships in abnormal group behavior. A redemptive process may be at work under the most distressing conditions.

The specialized training and skill of the pastoral psychologist in the mental hospital has also been more actively employed in recent years. Programs of group action and psychodrama have been used to help restore relationships among those who have retreated from life and its meaning. The initial impulse of the pastoral care movement emerged from the mental hospital, much of the clinical training program has been centered there, and much of the most significant work has emerged from the work of those who apply their special skills to this highly refined form of pastoral care.

Another form of specialized community exists on the college campus, where hundreds of thousands of young people are moving through the adjustment from home to independent living in society. In addition to the chaplain appointed by the institution there are often pastoral counselors who do specialized religious work through denominational auspices. Again a specialized parish is set up to do work with a limited group in a limiting setting.

A final form of specialized pastoral care has developed in recent years through the appointment of chaplains to industry. This again is an effort to move out of the religious institution into the daily life and needs of people. Combining the insights of psychology, sociology and economics, the industrial chaplain works where the stresses of family, work and personal conflict create crises. Each of these specialized forms of pastoral care has moved well beyond the traditional bounds of the parish to minister to those needs that are within the field of interest and competence of the pastoral psychologist. Much of this special type of ministry has developed in the last few decades as a part of the increased use of specialization as a way of implementing the human concerns of the pastor.

As we look at the impact of these specialized forms of pastoral care we find that the movement has made important contributions to the more traditional work of the parish ministry in at least three ways. It has stimulated special education, has discovered new meanings in rites, rituals and ceremonies, and has refined techniques in individual and group counseling.

These insights of pastoral psychologists have tended to modify the content and direction of adult education programs. The movement has been away from the historical and Biblical material toward self-discovery and the application of psychological insight to daily living. Some of the leaders in sensitivity training have been pastoral counselors. The trend is illustrated in two denominational adult study books I was asked to write twelve years apart. The first was *This Is My Faith* and the second, a little more than a decade later, *Facing Ourselves*.

This has also affected the concept and content of preaching, always a specialized form of pastoral communication in the parish. A traditional form of adult education, in the past it has been largely exhortation, starting with a picturing of the hazards of sinful living, then appeal to neurotic guilt feelings, and finally a challenge to accept a quick and simple solution to the problem. The fear of punishment often played a large part in the message, and the dramatic skill of the preacher was tested by his ability to make his hearers uncomfortable enough with themselves to be motivated toward the new self that was acceptable from the point of view of the doctrinal tenets of the particular church and preacher.

Much was added to the pastoral counseling movement by Dr. Harry Emerson Fosdick who went through a mental and emotional crisis. Because of his own personal interest he was concerned with helping people cope with life creatively. His person-centered approach to preaching and his use of psychological insight in sermons had an important influence on all subsequent preaching, acknowledged or not. Persons were challenged to grow in maturity, responsibility and insight into their own motives and the behavior of others. He used historical material and Biblical illustrations to illuminate the psychological and spiritual truths he interpreted. His emphasis was increasingly positive rather than negative, and people were invited to move toward self-fulfillment and the more abundant life rather than threatened by punishment and sent away more filled with fears than when they had come.

Even in relation to children there has been a change in emphasis due to pastoral psychology. The modification of educational materials for children has been influenced by the findings of the child development researches of Piaget and Gisell. Instead of teaching children doctrine and history, the emphasis has turned toward individual development and group understanding. With the growing recognition of the fact that maturity is less taught than achieved, the emphasis is now more on doing and being than on learning and affirming. With this modification of educational approach there is an increased emphasis on parent education, for it is clearly recognized that parents are ultimately the chief teachers of values and attitudes by either direction or indirection. Many of the changes that have grown from the pastoral psychology movement have been slow and gradual, implicit rather than explicit. However, when measured over four decades of active influence the changes have been considerable and the process, well begun, is continuing to exert a considerable influence.

One of the important influences of the pastoral psychology movement has been the research that has led to a new understanding and appreciation of the psychological function of rites, rituals and ceremonies. Here the influence of Gorer, Jung, Abt, May and Progoff has been significant.

Much of traditional religious practice has employed simple or more complicated rites and rituals that have accumulated with time, have appeared to be largely nonrational in meaning, but have channeled large amounts of emotion. Those ritualized forms of behavior usually accreted about highly emotional experiences in life. They were modifications of dedication rites at birth, induction rites at puberty, ceremonial rites at marriage, social events relating to war, group leadership, or threats to social viability, and to death.

Lawrence Abt in *Acting Out* has brought together important insights about the use of established and newly created means of expressing those deep and potentially damaging emotions that cannot easily be put into words. This can involve the acting out of creative or destructive feelings. And the health of society and the individual members of it may be more than we usually recognize dependent on the availability of significant ways of working through or acting out the deeper emotions. Lloyd Warner has verified this in relation to larger national and social events. So the value of the rites, rituals and ceremonials may not be apparent at the conscious or rational level, but that only makes it more likely that important but subconscious or unconscious needs are being met.

Traditional religion, while it has varied considerably in doctrine and organizational life, has had a common practice of worship, the process of giving worth to life. Often to the uninitiated observer the processes have appeared to be without meaning or rational import, but to the initiated there has been security in the process where individuals could emphasize their individuality and be alone with their own deepest thoughts at the same time that they were supported by a group that understood their needs and shared the quest in the presence of common symbols and shared emotions.

The more rationalistic religious groups tended to reduce or eliminate these rites and rituals. Quakers, Unitarians, Universalists and New Thought groups sought to develop a tradition that was largely without ceremony and substituted a direct appeal to the intellect. But their growth has been small, perhaps because they failed to recognize the emotional needs that were being satisfied by the opportunities for acting out.

Goeffrey Gorer, the British anthropologist, in his recent study of British death attitudes has arrived at some conclusions that are important for pastoral care, especially in the parish. He points out that our largely death-denying, death-defying culture has tried to defeat death by making out it does not exist. This has led to an elimination of many of the ceremonial events that had traditionally channeled the powerful emotions that accompany acute deprivation. However, the elimination of the ceremonial events tended to produce strong anxiety, varied forms of maladaptive behavior, a fear of emotional expression that Gorer called "mummification" and a loss of the capacity to love in healthful and self-fulfilling ways. He identified forms of destructive behavior in the individual as suicidal or partially suicidal in groups as an increase in vandalism and the makeshift rituals of meaningless destruction. His conclusion was that the more ceremonial involvement there was at the time of death, the more quickly the persons worked out their feelings and returned to normal living. The denial of the ritualized behavior tended to produce abnormalities in emotion and action that projected themselves indefinitely into the future so that the personalities were changed toward neuroticism and generalized forms of distress.

Lloyd Warner and Robert Fulton, sociologists, have added their insights to those of Gorer and Abt in supporting the personal and social significance of providing healthful channels for acting out the emotional crises of life. The pastor in the parish, then, is not concerned with eliminating this group activity that does not always appear rational, but rather seeks to understand the emotional needs and superrational meanings that are being met, and to enrich them by providing more not less, and replacing the unacceptable with that which is more currently valid.

May and Progoff in their studies of symbolism in religion and literature have thrown new light on the psychological significance of old and familiar words that speak not only with the weight of the words themselves but also with a weight of emotional meaning that comes from the enrichment of words by tradition and psychological overtones that cannot be measured by ordinary yardsticks of meaning.

Jerome Frank's study of authority in medical practice implies that a comparable process may be at work with religious words and practices that can exert a compelling influence upon life just because the words are enriched by the authority of tradition and the insistent emotional needs of those who are overborne by the struggle to cope with the mystery of meaning in their own consciousness. The parish counselor cannot escape his obligation to re-examine the emotional meaning of old ways of doing things and old ways of saying things, for they may carry therapeutic values that have been obscured by the demands of merely rational judgment. Part of his function may be to restore those modes of communication to their rightful place in group life, or at least provide more valid and acceptable substitutes.

The pastor has always served as a physician of the soul and as a spiritual guide. Now the tools for his task have been refined and sharpened by those working in other disciplines in other forms of community. Yet parish counseling because it has different presuppositions about the nature of man and multiple relationships between the pastor and his people, which make the sterilized clinical setting difficult if not impossible to duplicate in the parish, and because the dynamics of the relationship are such that spontaneity and rapid movement may characterize it, is more adventurous and demanding.

This is true because in many instances the counseling process goes on without the people knowing it. The pastor meets his people not only in the counseling room but also in ceremonial events, in crisis situations, in hospital corridors, on the golf course, on the fishing trip, in the committee meeting and at the casual events of group life. His perception into the needs of people gives many direct and indirect opportunities for the special type of counseling he can provide. He is seldom able to be non-directive or eductive, even if he wants to be, for he is invested with a role and authority that is continually supplementing his nature as a person.

For many people the pastor is more of a personage than a person and he must always cope with this dimension of his relationship with added awareness and adequate compensation. He is expected to do and be certain things, and this expectation is part of his resource in working with people. Whether it is a liability or an asset depends on his skill in assessing his role and relationship with his people.

He carries an authority that moves in many directions at once, and he must find out what the concept of his authority is in the mind of his counselee before he determines the meaning of the relationship that exists. He in effect has much of his relationship structured by factors beyond his control before he enters into it, and therefore must function within it with different presuppositions and attitudes from his colleagues in clinical or institutional settings. But what may appear to be a hazard in some ways becomes a resource in other ways, and it is his ability properly to assess the role and relationship he possesses that gives to parish counseling both its unique discipline and its unusual opportunities.

The role of the parish counselor, then, may be different from other forms of counseling, but it has been enriched by the experience of colleagues who do their work in institutions or have done their research in clinics. His contact with his people may be more varied, but the demands on his skills are more exacting. He has to adapt and adjust to circumstances without delay, because the moment he has may be lost forever if it is not used with insight and skill.

Chapter 4

Finding a Model

As we have seen, the developments in the personality sciences have done much to modify concepts of pastoral care. Because we have been so close to these developments we may have some trouble in being completely objective about what has taken place. Perhaps other forces have made their contribution to changing concepts of pastoral care without our being aware of what has been happening. No one aspect of the social process can stand in isolation from all the rest.

It is quite impossible to reduce or simplify what has been taking place in our society and do justice to the wide variety of responses that we observe. But it may serve our purpose in this exploration to try to make some general classifications of major influences on parish counseling that are completely separated from religion or psychology. This we would do under three headings: first, the industrial model, second, the clinical model, and third, the pastoral model.

As we well know, the industrialization of society has had its influence in many directions, examined and unexamined. The examined changes have been approached in terms of the more materialistic and statistical measurements we apply to so much of living. We speak of progress as evidenced by increased productivity, and the state of our economic life shows its pulse through the gross national product. If the GNP is up, society must be in a healthy state, and if it is down we are in trouble. But at best this can be a superficial form of measurement and can touch only a portion of the social health that concerns us.

The effect of this type of measurement tends to depersonalize life and increase impersonal attitudes toward human beings. It is quite true that this was not the intent of industrialization, but the subtle influence of industrial progress produces its inevitable by-products. Just as industrial proficiency and accelerated productivity make more things for people, they also create problems for people such as shortages of natural products and contamination of air, land and water.

The two main contributions of industrialization were the enclosing of the means of production under roofs so that the age-old problems of coping with the elements could be controlled and the bringing of the work to the worker.

From the beginning of time man had to contend with nature. A farmer could work all year only to see his crops destroyed by a blight, a hailstorm or some other natural phenomenon. With the moving of industrial production indoors, it was possible to control climate and create optimal conditions for work with heat in winter and air conditioning in summer. But it tended to destroy man's sense of relationship to nature and its influences. Man not only was unresponsive to the impact of nature in this industrial setting but also was allowed to lose sight of the cosmic dimensions of his being.

God all too often became remote and meaningless, but the plant owner was all-important. He controlled life and destiny. Instead of organizing churches to implore God for favors, men organized unions to impress the corporation with needs and demands. As the corporation became more and more efficient it tended to be less and less humane, for the computers took over calculations and the human elements could get lost in the process. The power of the industrialist and the corporation grew, and the role of the individual became less personal and less significant.

As work was brought to the place of work, other factors like transportation and communication grew in significance, and the individual's status and control became less and less. From the beginning of time the worker had gone to his work. The farmer went out into the fields, the fisherman went off to the sea, and the hunter into the woods and fields. Now that was all to be changed. The work was brought to him in controlled circumstances. The assembly line was set at a speed to demand the most of the worker, and if one should fall by the wayside another was immediately put into his place so that the conveyor belt need not stop in its journey to the goal of its production. So the assembly line had a life of its own, and the worker on the line became more mechanical in his action and less human in his own eyes.

The factory and the industrial center became the new focal point of life. The magnitude of this influence on changed ways of life can be revealed by statistics. In the year 1900 seven of ten persons lived in rural areas. In 1970 seven of ten live in cities. Life has moved from the land where it was close to nature and elemental things to the industrial complex where it is separated from man's ancient roots. The problems of adjustment have been great and the dislocation of values, life styles and loyalties has confused where it has not confounded.

The industrial model has made its influence felt in many ways for good or ill. The small country school has been superceded by the educational industrial center, where the teacher presides on the assembly line and millions of children ride the conveyor, the school bus, to the place where education is the often impersonally dispensed product. Classes come to the teacher every hour on the hour, and the individualized relation often falls by the wayside. No one would say that there may not be improved educational methods employed to create the product-educated children but while facts may be conveyed the personal dimension that is essential to the creating of values may well be lost.

The industrial model can be seen also in what we call health delivery systems, a term borrowed from industry. Highly sophisticated equipment is brought together in one place, and highly trained personnel preside over the equipment. Patients are brought from far and wide to the big clinics and health care centers. The old family physician who knew his people and saw them in their homes has gone. Instead of the personalized housecall there is now the impersonal information sheet filled out by someone never seen before and in all probability never again.

The patient goes to a specialist who treats a disease rather than a person with a disease. In the course of a day in a clinic a patient may be examined by several specialists, who are more apt to consult x rays, blood test results and analyses of body by-products than engage in discussion of thoughts and feelings with a person who has feelings. On the basis of sophisticated analysis a program of treatment will be arrived at that may be sound in terms of medical science but leaves much to be desired as far as the human need is concerned. As a person is treated more and more impersonally, his apprehension and anxiety grow, and although his body may be wisely treated his sacred precincts of being may be ignored.

The industrial need has affected the parish ministry. The building boom of churches in the last generation has left pastors talking of their "plants" and their "industrial complexes" with functional usings to which people are brought to experience the products that are created there. Few are the new churches that do not boast a counseling room with the prescribed furniture and the decor that is designed to give soft light, stimulating art and a mood of wise and professional concern for pastoral care. If a person has a problem he goes to the secretary, who arranges for him to share an hour in this special room for purposes that are specifically determined by a philosophy of ministry and an industrial designer. The product is pastoral care, the suffering person is the consumer, and the counseling schedule is the conveyer belt.

The counseling interview may be taped for later study and

analysis, usually with the counselee's knowledge and consent. The basic elements of industrialization are acceded to with the work being brought to the pastor in the protected setting that may make it unnecessary to be concerned about any divine process at work. The professional attitude may be emphasized by the framed evidence of learning hanging on the wall. The patient knows he is in the presence of an authority. So he comes not so much as a person to share a human concern as he does as a part of a never ending chain of those troubled and in anguish who stop here for their fair share of a treatment process that may have impersonal elements about it.

Whether or not we admit it, we have all been more subject to the industrial processes than we like to admit. Its subtle influences determine how we meet people and how we treat them. Are there elements in this model that are unacceptable or need to be re-examined? Are there other models that might better serve the purposes of the pastor at work with people in the parish?

There is the clinical model, for one. It has proved its efficiency in health care delivery systems. It gives better treatment for physical ills, even though it may not be quite as folksy and personal. The pastor who has been largely trained in the great institutions of medical care may well feel more at home in this setting, for he knows its authority and recognizes its power at work.

Some of the best writing in the pastoral care movement has emerged from the clinical setting. Some of the most useful skills have been developed in the atmosphere of clinical procedures and attitudes. Why then should anyone question the validity of this model for the pastor?

The questions emerge at the point where the parish is a different way of encountering people. The clinic has its own authority, demands its own skills and provides its own benefits. The parish has a different authority, requires perhaps greater skills and provides its forms of intervention in the lives of people with a different mood and different attitudes toward acceptance.

In the clinic the persons come for a specific purpose and actively engage in the process. They do the traveling, they pay the bills, and they provide the time and energy involved in the clinical process. In the parish there may be a generalized malaise waiting to be explored. The perceptive pastor may have to encourage or stimulate the encounter that will make the exploration possible. There may be resistance to be overcome, fears to be allayed and attitudes to be prepared, and it may need to be done so carefully that the persons involved are unaware of the full meaning of the process.

In the clinic the professional person employs the skills he has learned usually in the clinical atmosphere. He is comfortable with where he is and the skills he is using. Usually he is supported by the resources and authority of an institution with status. The parish counselor may be obliged to develop new skills or adapt those learned in other settings for the more subtle and demanding tasks of the parish. The pastor may be working alone in an atmosphere that lacks authority or institutional support, and the only resources may be those of his own personality. In his encounter with people he may be obliged to put all there is of himself on the line without means of escape or any protection other than his own inner resources.

Usually the industrial or clinical model, valuable as it may be in other contexts, falls short of the needs of the pastor at work in the everyday encounters of the parish. His more useful model might be referred to as the pastoral model. He builds it himself out of three differing sources, the Biblical, the professional and the personal.

The very title pastor carries the implication of the pastoral role, that he has a special concern for a special group of people who are peculiarly his responsibility. While there may be those who wander in and out of his life, most of his time and energy will be used in working with those of his parish. If the image of the shepherd is used, they would be his flock. They are apt to be members of his congregation or related to it. They are people he knows in other life experiences. He may have been related to them through priestly, friendly or other human contacts that amplify his pastoral role. In a sense he works for them and they may feel a proprietary interest in him, for they help provide his home and pay his salary.

The shepherding concept has Biblical roots. There are also a variety of Biblical illustrations that clarify the meaning and practice of this role.

In his relation to the women at the well in Samaria Jesus moved toward an isolated and troubled person. He broke through the barriers of race, tradition, guilt and common practice to relate to her in such a way that she was changed. When there were people who were untouchable because of loathsome disease He went to them and reached out to touch them, to welcome them back into the human race. When there were insane people who were excluded from the community because of their behavior He went to them and sat down to talk with them as if in spite of their problems they were still entitled to human relationship. He thought it was tragic to be separated from the roots of human life, whether by accident, as the lost coin, or by circumstances, as with the lost sheep, or by deliberate and willful action, as with the prodigal son. When there were those excluded by their behavior, like the women caught in unacceptable behavior, He was slow to condemn and quick to defend, so that new opportunities could be found for a more valid existence. In all the ways we can imagine He sought to move toward people, and help them discover their resources for wise and useful living.

One of the rich opportunities that the pastor has in the parish approach to counseling is that he can move toward people. He does not have to wait for that percentage of the troubled who will make an appointment and come to him. He has the privilege of the shepherd who moves among his sheep and is known by them and respected and trusted by them. The pastor has a unique resource known as the pastoral call. No other professional has this privileged opportunity for relationship. Other professionals have to be called as they are needed. The pastor can use his sensitivity to be aware of need and move toward those who may be injured, sensitive and unable to break through their own hesitancy and fear to seek help.

But the pastor would not abuse this Biblical image, for he realizes that it carries with it important obligations. The pastor seeks to be the most highly disciplined and best-trained person that he can be. He may be available and approachable, but he is

never unprepared to cope with life, for he is the adequate professional. He brings to his work with people the best educational
endowment he can provide and the most up-to-date understanding he can develop of the human situation and his relation
to it.

As a professional he knows his strength and his weakness, his
skills and his inadequacies, and he does not bluff his way
through the important human encounters that are a part of his
parish life. He so respects the people he serves that if he cannot
adequately provide for their needs he seeks further help for
them. In fact part of his skill and some of his resource may be in
his ability to make referral wisely when needed.

In addition to a Biblical image and a professional role the
parish pastor realizes that his own faith and his own dedication
are basic resources in his work with people. A pastor whose
main impulse is to manipulate and control people for his own
purposes is bad news in human relations. The pastor who is so
insecure that he must always prove that he is right may have
some following among others who are insecure, but he will not
meet the needs of the people who would "grow in wisdom, and
in stature and in favor with God and man."

An agitated pastor cannot create the mood of calmness and
objectivity. The petulant or aggressive pastor will not create the
mood of trust that will bring people to him for understanding
and help. The threatened pastor who is always feeling under at-
tack will not be apt to bring trust and confidence to those who
seek it.

One of the important disciplines with those who enter into the
emotional and spiritual recesses of the lives of others is to have
his own house in order. This calls for maturity, self-discipline
and personal courage. It is not easy to be a counselor in the parish, for it is more difficult to hide the human weaknesses there.
The more than ordinary dedication and skill that is required to
be a parish counselor, however, places a person where he has the
opportunity to carry on a more broad-based and adventurous
ministry in the lives of those who come and those who do not
come, those who seek and those who must be sought.

No pastoral image is quite good enough that does not examine its origins carefully or assess its goals with clarity. The mere fact that an industrial image is prevalent in other disciplines does not make it automatically valid for the pastor. Just because others gain status and security in a clinical image, that does not mean it is good enough for the broader encounter the pastor has with his people.

Unless his image is rooted in a worthy tradition, honed by adequate training and continued mental growth, and fulfilled in personal commitment, the pastor in the parish may deny himself some of the most rewarding fruits of his work with people.

Chapter 5

A Theological Base for Counseling

Parish counseling is a specialized form of pastoral counseling. All pastoral counseling starts with a special conceptual base that employs theological assumptions about the nature of man and his relationship to the universe.

Other forms of counseling may have little philosophical base. They may be strong on technique and at the same time harbor quite pessimistic attitudes toward man and his nature. They may be built around clinical skills and important personal disciplines and yet feel that man is essentially a complicated mechanism that has no cosmic dimensions to his being.

The pastor at work among his people has quite a different orientation. He proclaims a faith that is based on the assumption that man's unique consciousness has a relationship to cosmic consciousness, and that the God-man relationship has deep significance not only for the endowment of life but also for the ways the endowment is used to bring life to fulfillment.

Man is a mystery. His capacity for creativity and for destructiveness seems to know no bounds. The struggle between good and evil impulses that rages within his being is not easily resolved. In the tradition of pastoral care man is seen in the midst of this struggle with the way he will go determined by a variety of influences, not the least of which is the theological orientation of the individual.

What man gives his highest loyalty to seems to be a major factor in directing the course of his life. If he is dedicated to the mere satisfying of appetites he may destroy himself and in the process injure or destroy others. If he finds a higher motivation, some cause or loyalty to which he can direct his major energies, he may develop nobility of character and as a by-product find the self-fulfillment that can enrich his life and give his spiritual development a significant direction.

Man is a developing creature. Beyond the mystery that surrounds his endowment and his creative capacity there is a clear understanding of some of the forces that can work to help him grow into a mature, sensitive person with balance and direction. He knows who he is and is aware of the direction in which he moves.

It is at this point that some theological presuppositions become important. Man is capable of great and audacious assumptions about his nature. The history of religious insight is filled with the great insights man has achieved concerning his own nature. He thinks of himself as made a little lower than angels in the order of creation. He thinks that he is worthy of cosmic recognition, that God in His creative wisdom is concerned with his development and has made the risk of granting freedom as an expression of faith in man. But God's faith in man appears to remain unfulfilled unless man has a faith in God's purpose. This faith in God's purpose gives man the goals and the incentives to work toward these goals. He feels that in a partnership with the divine he is involved in a struggle to achieve the final triumph of righteousness.

In this partnership there are shared responsibilities. Man does not appear to be able to do it all by himself, for the forces against which he struggles are too powerful. And God cannot defeat His purposes in giving man freedom by taking it away in order to accomplish His purpose. So what God cannot do without man, man cannot do without the heroic faith that is his commitment to God's purpose at work through him.

Man's commitment to God is activated by what has been traditionally called the indwelling of the Holy Spirit. In a sense this indwelling power to achieve is man's portion of God. If God is characterized in New Testament terms as forms of energy, light, power, spirit, truth and love, it is reasonable that the power of the spirit at work in man will stimulate these forms of energy in his being to fulfill the possibilities of his inner kingdom.

Too often men have thought of God in limited and limiting terms. The divine energy has been thought of as static and fixed, which on the face of it is contradictory. No analogy is adequate in speaking of the ultimate. Early in man's quest for a relationship to cosmic purpose man knew he could not reduce that cosmic nature to fit his small equipment for conceptualization. So early in the Jewish tradition no name was to be given to God. Rather, words were used that indicated the direction toward the holy of holies or, in more modern times, the ground of our being.

Where religious concepts have been limiting and bound by the threatened nature of the believer, this smallness has been projected in fear, judgment and preoccupation with sin and failure. Where religious concepts have been moved by the larger energizing forces within the relationship of the being and the Being, there has emerged a warmth, a love, an understanding that moves beyond judgment to a shared desire to help each other discover the fullest possibility in each other.

The pastor as counselor enters into this process of mutual self-discovery as one who seeks to mediate the healing, redeeming love of God. He does not compel, but he does respond. He does not command, but he does guide. He does not manipulate, but he does respect the moving spirit at work within another and serves as a midwife of ideas and a nurturing force in the often tender and hesitant growth of the spirit.

All pastoral care is the activating of the portion of God that is in the pastor in relation to and in respect for the portion of God that is in the life of the person he encounters.

Instead of being a static thing, it is a dynamic force at work. The tripartite nature of God is process and not a fixed point in a theological construct. The concept of God is the source of the powers that we perceive to be the nature of God. The historical revelation is the point where the abstract becomes real, and the spiritual enactment becomes the point where the potential of man becomes actualized by the indwelling of the Spirit.

While no analogies are adequate to bring to mind the true nature of God, analogies may be useful in making the process of relationship more tenable. If I were to speak the word *rose*, it would call to mind a genus of flowers. The variety of perception might be as varied as the minds that respond to the verbal stimulus. The word is not a flower, and in and of itself it never can be. However, if I handed you a flower and told you it was a rose, the genus would come alive in the specific revelation of the individual flower. Yet another dimension of comprehension of the meaning of a rose is found at the point where the five apertures to consciousness respond. You smell the rose, see the rose, feel the rose, and can even taste it if you wish. While it is difficult to hear a silent object, it would be possible to rub the rose against your ear and verify in another form its individualized existence. So the nature of God beyond our conceiving has been brought into our consciousness by a unique revelation and our personalized experience of the power through the indwelling of the Holy Spirit.

More abstractly, we might speak of the components of the nature of God in New Testament terms. "God is light and in Him is no darkness at all." We all know what light is in practical terms, but in purely scientific terms we are not in total agreement. Is light manifest in a flow of particles or in a pulsing radiation of waves? Can a person look at the sun, or can a person hold a part of the sun in his hand? The puzzling questions may not be answered in the final form by abstractions but rather in personal experience. The sun is a source of the earth's energy. The light we possess comes from the sun. It need not come to us now directly. We have learned to take the light of the sun that was stored up in the earth millions of years ago as coal and oil and transform it into the energy that can be easily carried about in the dark to penetrate it with beams of light. An oil lamp or an electric lightbulb is the evidence of this transformation. And when you go into a dark closet with a flashlight you are holding a part of the sun in your hand. Surely it is not all of the sun, but it is of the sun, nonetheless. And so with the Holy Spirit at work in a man. Certainly it is not all the power of God, but it is of God. And it is at work in man, and it can illuminate a darkened soul and redirect the misused energy of life. It is God at work in man.

The role of the parish counselor is to meet people in the darkened closets of life, in the places where their energy has been misdirected, and be instrumental in helping to discover a new power, a new purpose and a new energy that can bring the power of God into the life of the individual.

How does the pastor counseling in the parish fulfill this purpose of bringing the power of God into the lives of persons? What are the resources available to him and the skills he can employ to that end?

In the first place the parish counselor is a form of living theology. In his own life he is constantly trying to bring three forms of energy into creative expression. He believes in the forward motion of life, of its movement toward goals of personal fulfillment. This is comparable to kinetic energy. This is the movement of life toward health when there is illness or injury. It is the healing process at work. It is the basic drive of life waiting to be expressed and directed.

A second form of energy is the potential that exists not only in the drive of life toward its goals but also in the ability of life to self-consciously select its goals and with deliberation move toward them. This is reflected in commitment and in dedication with all of the energy of life that is employed to these ends.

There is also the actual energy where the kinetic and the potential are brought into active relationship in the process of living. This is where a person uses the drive of life and the potential of faith to achieve within himself the living fruits of his faith. The pastor in his own living seeks to make his faith a living thing that can believe in people so effectively that they want to believe in themselves more fully. But, of course, the basis for any such belief must be found in the fulfilled and fulfilling faith of the pastor at work in his inner being and in its expression toward the people he works with.

The pastor's commitment is not only a way of life. It is also a resource when he relates to the lives of others. They can quickly sense how deeply he feels with them. Those who are emotionally distressed are also apt to be emotionally sensitive. They have a kind of instant knowledge as to the sincerity and conviction of the person who relates to them. If he harbors resentment or hostility they may quickly pick it up. If he radiates loving concern and dedicated interest they seem to have a way of knowing it and responding to it.

This living theology cannot be feigned or artificially produced. If it is not real it does not exist as far as the intimate human relationship of counseling is concerned. For it to be a resource it must be real.

But the pastor is not only a form of living theology. He must be also a person with a competence to support his commitment. When he functions so close to the sacred precincts of personality he must have a deep respect for the inner being of others. He must recognize that there is also a living theology at work in the lives of those he encounters. If it is valid in him it is also valid in them. The same forms of energy that are brought together in his functioning are also operative in those with whom he works. While there may be a need for patience and skill in bringing it to full usefulness, his belief becomes a resource to that end.

His concern for the value of life demands that he treat it with the respect for its sacredness that is basic to his commitment. So he works to refine his insight into human psychological and spiritual processes. He seeks to develop his competence in the vital encounter that is implicit in every counseling relationship.

Whenever two people encounter each other in the important business of living, they do things to each other. They can inspire confidence or they can produce antagonism. They can fortify faith or stimulate doubt. They can undermine confidence or provide reassurance. The pastor as a living and vital resource is constantly engaged in producing reactions in the lives of the persons he touches. How skillful he is in managing his own life will inevitably have a bearing on how his people see him and respond to his ministry. If he is a sickly, withdrawn and uncertain person he is communicating his attitudes in all he is and says and does. If he is a symbol of strength and wisdom and understanding he is bound to have an impact on the lives of his people that will stimulate confidence and encourage healthful growth.

The theological assumptions the pastor has about the nature of man and God and the power of the Spirit to be at work in life is projected through the multiple roles the pastor lives among his people. It is the important base from which all else emerges. A sound theology of pastoral care becomes the philosophy of life the pastor employs in his ministry. So it is always important to look to the foundations, for if they are sand his program of pastoral care falls apart. If it is built on rock, though he may not be all-wise and skilled, his true concern will guide his life and show through all he does.

Chapter 6

The Counselor
Pays Attention to
His People

What is it a person does when he pays attention? Quite simply, he marshals all of his resources to be aware of another person and that person's communication.

The pastor may be able to pay attention better if he has developed some methods for working with people that can bring to bear some wisdom and some structure. Within the often casual nature of parish counseling it may well be that the counselee never knows that there is structure or method. But the pastor may find security in what he does if he employs some special ways of paying attention to those he encounters.

Every pastor practices pastoral psychiatry, the process of soul-healing. The very nature of his ministry and relation with people involves it. The problem is always whether or not he uses effective and helpful methods in his work with people. Is he a good or bad soul-healer? It is strange that the word *psychiatry*, which in its essence means soul-healing, should generally be considered to be the domain of the medical psychologist. The pastor does not want to trespass in areas where he is unfitted, but neither does he want to relinquish a ministry to souls that have always been his.

Perhaps his right as a worker with souls has been questioned because he had become so preoccupied with other things—rituals, organizations and causes—that he had failed to see the need of his people. Perhaps he had been so hesitant about using theories and principles that upset some of his traditional thinking that he had lost by default in the area of practical methods and procedures. Or he may have been afraid of the deeper significance of the newly discovered theories and principles and preferred to defend himself and his ideas rather than approach this new body of learning with a primary consideration for his people.

Whatever the reasoning may have been, a new generation is making the new way increasingly important for the pastor. He hears talk of different ways of counseling and wonders what this implies. If he keeps in mind that it is not so much what a method is called but what it is able to accomplish that serves the purpose, he will keep the counselee in focus, which is the important thing to do.

The types of counseling are referred to as directive, nondirective, eductive, family-centered, group-oriented, behavior-modifying and educational. A simple method for understanding the difference in the use of these methods may be indicated in a typical interview. The pastor starts with the patient or counselee and tries to determine the major area of the problem. If the problem is essentially emotional in character, he is wise to be nondirective in approach and to consider the possibility of referral if the disturbance seems to be rooted in lower levels of consciousness. If, on the other hand, the counselee's problem seems to be essentially intellectual in nature, where rational approaches may be indicated, such as choosing a vocation, a college or other areas where information is needed, the pastor may well be more directive and educational in approach. If he does not have the information or understanding to satisfy the counselee, he is again prepared to refer the person to one who is more apt to have the information needed. The pastor, however, is always on the alert for those emotional problems that are masked in the guise of the religious or intellectual question. To that end, he will usually follow the rule: When in doubt, be nondirective.

When the pastor understands his function, he is able to draw the lines in method more easily. The pastor has neither the purpose nor the function of the medical therapist. The pastor works within certain specific self-imposed limitations. In approaching a patient, the medical therapist is directive while the pastor is usually nondirective. The psychiatrist seeks a transference relationship while the pastor seeks to avoid it. The physician is manipulative while the pastor is nonmanipulative. Naturally the physician is able to prescribe medicine while the pastor does not. But the pastor is religious and uses the resources of religion where the medical doctor may not. The pastor is interested in the total personality, where the psychiatrist is interested essentially in the psyche. The pastor represents an organization, the church, whereas the physician is responsible primarily to a body of ideas. The doctor plays a single role, where the clergyman is obliged to play many roles. And the pastor is an active representative of a traditional and sacramental use of symbols that have significance for the soul, while the physician is not.

The medical psychotherapist has learned through a strenuous discipline to separate his own emotions from those of his patient. Quite in contrast, the pastor has been taught to use his emotions to fortify his witness. This is apt to create a danger in the counseling process, for the pastor through his words may be more inclined to reveal himself than to release the soul-binding forces in the life of the counselee. And the self the pastor may reveal, unless he has a deep insight into his own growth and nature, is apt to be filled with his own problems, antagonisms, fears and prejudices. He may reveal and pass along the limitations of his own understanding, his lack of grasp on reality and his poverty of knowledge of things beyond his own particular field of study.

For his own good and for the good of his counselees it would be wise for the pastor to have a good working knowledge of the criteria of maturity and normality. He would find a book by Dr.

Overstreet, *The Mature Mind,* a help in evaluating the degree of mental growth. Probably he could not find a better expression of this in psychiatric literature than in the chapter dealing with the ten criteria of normality and maturity found in the textbook written by Dr. Maurice Levine, titled *Psychotherapy in Medical Practice.* Here the pastor will find a yardstick to measure himself as well as to measure others.

With an understanding of the criteria of normality and a wise insight into the limitations and opportunities of his position as a pastoral counselor, the pastor will want some simple method for handling the pastoral interview. As was noted earlier, there can be no set formula for people do not fit into formulas, but there can be an easily adaptable procedure that will make for effectiveness and thoroughness. Some such approach as the four-step method indicated here may be helpful to the pastor whose experience has been limited and who has not as yet worked out his own approach.

First impressions can mean a lot to the perceptive counselor. Just by looking at a person he can begin to sense some of the symptoms. Of course, such conclusions should be tentative and acted upon only as they are supported by other corroborative information. The very approach of a person may be significant. One can note the meaning of a direct and confident approach as different from the hesitant and uncertain attitude. A warm, firm handshake can mean something quite different from the weak and clammy handshake of the recessive person, or the over-rigorous grasp of the compensating person. Dress also tells things about a person. A woman in severely tailored and masculine attire may be saying something about her attitude toward her sex, while the decidedly feminine attire may say quite the opposite. The concern for style and the attractiveness of the clothes may indicate something of the degree of self-esteem of the person, while slovenliness and lack of interest are apt to be indications of depression and low self-esteem.

The way a person sits down may have meaning. If he sits on the edge of his chair and looks all about the room as if fearful of an open door or an open window, it may mean quite the opposite from the attitude of the person who pushes his chair back and goes to open a door or a window. The muscle reactions of the person may reveal tension. The person who clasps and unclasps his hands and crosses and recrosses his legs is indicating something about his state of mind, just as if he used words. And the person who sits down calmly with composure and ease is saying quite the opposite in all probability.

Facial reactions may be especially significant. The long face with the turned down corners of the mouth often indicates pessimism and despondency, while the upturned corners of the mouth and crowsfeet about the eyes may indicate a healthful sense of humor. Just the quality of the countenance may indicate whether or not a person has a capacity for friendship and satisfactory social relations. The color of the skin and face say something. The sallow, gray and pale skin may indicate a neurotic tendency, while a florid, ruddy complexion may indicate something of the sustained emotional pressure under which a person lives. Fear and doubt may show through the eyes, and the person whose eyes are tense may indicate his inner tension and fear.

The voice also may be a barometer of feeling. The harsh, raspy and high-pitched voice is apt to indicate tension and anxiety, while the normal person's voice is usually well modulated and musical. The tongue and the lips also can indicate emotion that is suppressed. In these and other ways the alert counselor can gain an understanding of the emotional state of his visitor, even before any significant words are exchanged. Often the skill of the counselor in interpreting the unspoken expression of a person can determine the direction and helpfulness of an interview. Fast's *Body Language* and Ruesch's *Non-Verbal Communication* give added useful insights.

When conversation begins, the ability of the pastor to read between the lines, to listen with what Theodor Reik calls "the third ear," can go far in revealing the deeper and unspoken disturbances of the individual. The inclination to protest too much may be an unconscious effort to cover up a source of disturbance. The inability to remember certain salient factors in an experience may reveal where the soul injury lies. Slips of the tongue may reveal what a person really thinks but has been trying to keep from saying. A father who resented his daughter's marriage found it almost impossible to remember her married name. Such partial amnesia, like protesting too much, indicates areas of emotional tension, and the wise pastor is alert to the things that are said by indirection just as he weighs the meaning of things that are said directly. He will make careful note of all of these things and, though he probably does not mention such things in the interview, will use them for his own guidance in trying to understand and interpret the factors at work in the personality of the person he would help.

Second would be the effort to evaluate the symptoms that have been presented, directly and indirectly. The pastor seeks to find the answer to the persistent question "Why?" Here he weighs the evident stimuli against the evidences of personality disturbance to see whether or not the effect is reasonable in terms of the cause that is presented. For instance, on answering the door one evening I found a husky and usually well-possessed man in tears. He entered and seated himself, and for some moments he shook with sobs. He was unable, for a time, to say anything that was understandable. After the first few minutes, however, the condition gradually eased itself, and he was able to say, "When I went home after work tonight I found my mother dead on the floor. I came to you because I thought you could tell me what to do." Though I could not tell him what to do, I could help see him through the ordeal of the next few hours with all that they would involve. But more than that, I was able to evaluate his behavior in relation to the stimulus. His reaction was normal for him under such a circumstance. Had he acted like that at another time with no evident immediate emotional stimulus, I would have had reason to look further for the cause of the disturbance.

There are times when it is more difficult to assess the symptoms. Sometimes it is necessary to get further data to fill in the picture before the cause-effect relationship can be evaluated. A woman who came in a state of deep emotion directed against her husband could be a case to illustrate this point. Could her bitterness against her husband be a case of jealousy with all that is involved in its revealing suspicion, fear and insecurity? Or was the behavior of the husband a sufficient cause to warrant such a response on her part? It was quite obvious that she was hardly an adequate witness for both prosecution and defense, and so any evaluation of the symptoms would have to be delayed until more of the evidence was in. There are very few cases that are all black and all white, and the rule of caution is always wise to follow. It is better to be overcautious than to make the error of becoming a partisan in a situation where the best help can be given as an emotionally uninvolved counselor.

It is at this point that the importance of a personal history is evident. So as a third factor we should seek to gain some sort of working knowledge of the forces that were operative to shape the personality. Sometimes much of this information is available to the pastor in advance of the interview. At other times he can gain considerable information by listening carefully and fitting together the factors at work as he might the pieces of a jigsaw puzzle. At still other times he may be able to lead out, by careful rephrasing of statements and the use of judicious questions, the information that can supplement his understanding of the forces at work. He should not overlook the influence of childhood situations, for their influence can be great.

If the parents have been authoritarian the pastor may understand more easily the dependency of the children on the one hand or their unwise experimental behavior on the other. If there has been a long history of illness, that may be reflected in behavior and attitude, especially if the illness were during the formative years of childhood. Also, unusual home circumstances may reflect themselves in behavior. Students of child development say that children who have been cared for in foundling homes without adequate mother substitutes invariably grow up to have marked factors of seclusiveness about their personalities. Orphans tend to be aggressive in their behavior, to try to compensate for the losses they have suffered in emotional security through the years of childhood.

In getting the personal history it is also important to know about persistent frustrations. If a man has for years worked at a job he did not want, that may well be the cause of the outbreak of unreasonable behavior toward his family and friends. If a child has run away repeatedly in childhood it is a factor that needs to be considered in the total pattern of behavior in the adult, for the escape attitude toward reality can reflect itself in various ways, and a clue to traditional types of behavior may be indicative in the particular problem under consideration. For in approaching any one problem of emotional disturbance or behavior, it is invariably found that it is closely related to other kindred situations in the past. If some understanding of the past can be available for the pastor, he can have a better understanding of what to expect in the present. That knowledge is a valuable ally in his work of healing.

Each pastor will develop his own method of keeping records. Often a sort of personal code of abbreviations can be useful. It is important, in a pastoral counseling relationship that may run into many interviews, not to depend on the memory entirely. If before each interview the memory can be refreshed, it helps to keep the counselor alert to new factors that may enter the picture, as well as to those attitudes that may have been conditioned as a result of the relationship with the pastor.

Some men use tape recorders to make detailed records of each interview. This may be useful in getting a complete record and also in permitting a careful study of the counselor's technique in the interview. The obvious dangers, however, are that the counselee may discover that the interview is being recorded and become resistive. Or, if he knows in advance that a recording is being made, he may be so restrained in his attitude as to render the interview useless as far as real helpfulness is concerned. Individual circumstances will have to determine the use of mechanical recording devices, but expense and the large amount of time required to hear playbacks tend to make such methods difficult.

A simple record of the important elements of the interview can be jotted down in a few minutes and filed for future reference. Here a word of caution might be spoken, for it is easy for the undisciplined counselor to put into the record those items that suit his interest and his conditional analysis of the situation. Unless the record can be objective and honest, it may serve quite a different purpose from that intended. Here, of course, the mechanical recording is foolproof, though it does not record many of the little acts and attitudes that are caught by a trained eye and ear. The taking of careful personal histories will, however, indicate the need of some sort of careful record-making.

The fourth step in the method of parish counseling would be to try to ascertain the damage that may have been done to the personality and character structure of the individual through the tensions and other emotionally disturbing factors observed, and then to proceed with a plan of therapy. Medical doctors would call this diagnosis and prescription, but we would avoid thinking in such medical terms. We might think more simply in such terms as these: "How serious is the situation?" "What can be done about it?"

On the basis of the symptoms noted and evaluated and the personal history of the individual, something is required. This brings us to the most important point in the relationship, for it is at this point that we determine how we shall proceed in the future in dealing with the counselee. When presented in one, two, three, four fashion it may seem alarming to be brought to the places where some decision must be made determining the welfare of the individual who sits before you. But, in fact, no such situation is ever entered into without some such decision being made. To decide to do nothing is one type of answer, and its effects may be far-reaching. To fidget and fuss and be indecisive is another answer, and this may increase the disturbance of the counselee even more. But to set out on a definite course of action with well-defined objectives is yet another answer. And to indicate the advisability of referral is also a diagnosis and prescription.

Here again the analogy to the physician may be helpful if it does not become too definite a pattern. The physician, after getting the information that he thinks is essential to a diagnosis, determines whether he shall proceed with treatment, or whether he shall refer his patient to a specialist. If he is in a medical center with the specialists in the same building, he is able to make the decision of referral more easily than if he were a lonely country doctor hundreds of miles from a medical center. So he balances what is desirable with what is practicable. Circumstances compel him to accept responsibility in remote regions

that he would gladly delegate in a city. Much the same sort of
thing is true in the pastor's relationship with the counselee. Part
of the pastor's problem is that of determining what must be
done in the exact sort of circumstance within which he is operating at the given time. It is foolish to tell a disturbed person to
see a psychiatrist if the person is impoverished and the nearest
psychiatrist is working under a capacity load hundreds of miles
away. He must do the best he can at the time to minister to the
needy soul that is his responsibility. Quite different would be the
situation of a city pastor who happens to have a devout psychiatrist as a member of his parish with whom he is free to consult
at will, as well as a trained psychologist who is ready to assist
with projective tests. So circumstances inevitably determine any
program that the pastor will adopt.

The experience and competence of the pastor would also determine his procedure. A skilled pastor might work patiently
with a depressed person, seeking to relieve the emotional pressure that is indicated, while the inexperienced worker might offer a brief prayer and give a superficial bit of reassurance, and
send the person on his way with added reason for depression.
But in either case, the pastor would be following a therapeutic
program. The difference would be that one was competent and
probably effective, while the other was incompetent and perhaps
even dangerous. In medical terms, one might be called worthy
practice and the other quackery. The medical profession operates under a code that places high value on the life of each individual person, no matter what the circumstances may be. The
pastor cannot well operate on a program that shows less respect
for the soul of a man.

As a pastor develops mutual interests with other members of
caretaking professions he may enrich his own skills and provide
resources to his people that they might not find except through
his knowledge and interest.

Yes, not only does the pastor pay attention to people, but he
does it in a way that encourages disciplined awareness of his
privileged role with people and his strategic position in bringing
to those who have special needs those resources which represent
special skills.

Chapter 7

Partners and Purposes

No matter how lonely the role of the parish counselor may seem, there are persons within reach who can serve as partners in pastoral care. Sometimes they may not be within easy reach, but they can be sought out and wisely employed as the occasion warrants.

The team ministry has developed within recent years. It makes it possible for many persons dispersed to share the benefits of special skills. Clinics and counseling centers make the caretaking professionals more accessible. But even in remote regions there are resources available for those who work to discover them.

The pastor may find retired persons with special training who would be willing to give some of their time to serving the community. There may be resources in the educational system of the larger community that would work with him. Sometimes women who have been social workers move into the community as wives busy with their tasks in the family, but who would be willing to give some time to serving special needs in the community.

As he tries to develop a program for meeting the needs of members of his parish the pastor may discover rich resources in the community that he was unaware of. He may find that community, state and federal agencies are prepared to cope with some of the anxiety-creating problems of his people. Often some of the financial burden for special care can be met by agencies and endowments that are available. Sometimes the pastor's function may be to interpret to the pride-stricken individual that he is well within his rights in making claims upon such funds. Also the pastor will find that the average social worker is by both training and inclination a considerate and reasonable counselor who takes pride in helping meet the psychological as well as the physical needs of his clients.

When it comes to the community program as it affects the mental and emotional life of the individual, the pastor will find in most communities a branch of the Mental Health Association. This organization with its child guidance clinics, its projective testing equipment, group therapy and individual psychiatric services is a dependable referral agency, although usually its capacities are taxed to the limits. Usually the Family Society, or its equivalent, has on its staff a psychiatric social worker trained to counsel in the emotional problems that affect family life. Where alcoholism may be a problem, state commissions on alcoholism are staffed to give psychiatric aid and psychological counseling. In many cities and towns Alcoholics Anonymous is ready and willing to help with its ministry to alcoholics.

In helping to determine his program in the community, the pastor will want to know in advance what agencies are available. Also he will want to know precisely what they can be expected to do. It is disturbing to a counselee to be unwisely referred, and then find further frustration in being sent from pillar to post trying to get the aid that was promised him. Usually a telephone call will suffice to get the information the pastor needs in such matters. And he will find that in most cases he will be treated with the understanding and courtesy that would be shown to other professionals working in the field. Most social workers seem pleased to have the cooperation of competent clergy and will in turn prove to be wise and helpful allies within the parish.

Perhaps it would be wise for the pastor to know something of the training and approach that the social worker takes. For his own good it might be wise to have studied carefully, and have at hand for ready reference, such a textbook as Dr. Lawson G. Lowrey's *Psychiatry for Social Workers.* The pastor may feel disinclined to serve on committees of various social agencies, but he will find that the chance to know and understand the capabilities and programs of these community agencies in the fields related to his needs as a counselor will well repay such time as he invests in them. And further, he will be able to bring to such agencies the richer insights of the Christian view of personality that sometimes seem to be lacking.

Ascertaining the damage to the person and establishing a program to meet the need of the individual is a major assignment. It calls for care, training and resourcefulness. No two cases can be treated in quite the same manner, and no case can be treated lightly.

The pastor must also be prepared for the indirect opportunities of counseling. Often those who need his aid are least apt to seek it out. Then he may be obliged to work through the family and friends of such persons. It may be that he can interpret to parents of a difficult adolescent the dynamics of behavior at that stage of growth. He may be able to help a nagging wife to see her relationship to the behavior of her often intoxicated husband. He may be able to explain the dynamics of behavior to the family of the neurotic individual so that they will not add further fuel to the already raging fire within, but will be able instead to serve a helpful and healing function.

The pastor who is the helpful shepherd is not only ready to aid those whose difficulty has become acute, but he also watches over his flock to be aware of those who may be wandering. He is aware of those who may be finding it difficult to identify themselves with the group where the normal desires for life and work and fellowship may be satisfied. He may sense the feeling of a person who wants friendship but seems unable either to give or receive it. Such a person may be in danger of falling into a human relationship that will be exploited and injurious. His concern for the physical and social welfare of his people not only keeps him close to them, and them close to him, but also serves the preventative function of relieving tensions and strains on personality while they are yet amenable to the type of ministrations that are well within the range of competence and propriety for the parish counselor.

It might be wise to sum up in a paragraph the important items for a pastor to keep in mind as he works out a program of pastoral work for his parish. In counseling with people he keeps himself out of the picture wherever the counselee's resources are available and adequate. He keeps the emotional content of his relationship at a minimum for there is usually too much emotion at work already. He seeks to establish empathy, rapport, resonance, a sense of oneness with the troubled person. In his counseling he remains calm, relaxed, unshocked and adequate emotionally. He is slow to interpret, for he knows his function is not so much to reveal his own knowledge as to help release the counselee's resources and insight. He is wise enough to know that the problem of emotional disturbance is not helped by intellectual understanding as much as it is by the total being organizing for a new program of action in its personal and social relationships.

Then, too, the pastor remembers that his function is to be a specialist in health of mind and spirit. He does not become so absorbed in the abnormal that normal people will fail to approach him for fear of being labeled. He keeps himself accessible to persons of all ages and in all states of life. He is professional in behavior, yet personal and friendly without being forward. He breathes the dignity of one whose respect for others is not superficial but is, rather, basic to his whole view of life. He is careful to use the language that is a bridge of understanding rather than a barrier to real communion of minds. Where he uses humor it is as a solvent rather than as an effort to amuse or be clever. His belief in the sacredness of human personality becomes the determinant of his relation with people, and his attitude is communicated more by his behavior in every situation than by his words. He breathes the concern and compassion that raises the self-esteem of the defeated, the confidence of the depressed and the hope of the forlorn. Yet it is not by superficial words but by genuine concern that this is done.

When the pastor realizes the importance of his counseling ministry, he seeks to be adequately prepared for it. Some of this preparation can be done through his private study. It is for such a purpose that the annotated bibliography is appended. Others will be able to give time to brief courses in the field or take clinical work of one type or another that can give practice under supervision in the counseling techniques. Still others will take specialized training in student days to prepare themselves more adequately for their work with people.

Knowing what to do gives confidence to the pastor, where ignorance adds to his confusion. For instance, a pastor who stands helpless before the drunk who has knocked at his door feels hopelessness. He may abuse this guilt-stricken human by sending him away or by adding to his guilt with a sermon. But if he can invite him in, get him to drink a quart of milk, take a few salt tablets and a couple of high-potency vitamin capsules, he will find that in a half hour or so he has a different person on his hands, one who is able to respond to his words and who appreciates his considerate handling of him when he came downcast and needy. So the pastor seeks the knowledge and information that can be his tools in meeting the real situations of life.

Yet never does he forget that his basic approach to people is religious in motivation and in content. With the prayerful George Muller he knows that "the beginning of anxiety is the end of faith, and the beginning of true faith is the end of anxiety." So he keeps that faith forever foremost. For it not only sustains him but is his basic belief in maintaining his high estimate of others. Sometimes he may feel that faith cannot take the place of training, and it should not be obliged to, but he has no reason to stand before the psychiatrist with a feeling of inferiority. They represent two disciplines and two approaches to the mystery of the human soul. In the final analysis the theories of the medical psychologist are essentially a frame of reference to give meaning to the phenomena of life, and so also is religion, except that religion is oriented to a supranatural focus. Hear the testimony of a noted psychotherapist and teacher at Oxford who had himself been psychoanalyzed: "I have become more convinced than ever that religion is the most important thing in life, and that it is essential to mental health."

The man of religion may in the final analysis be the true scientist. Centuries before Christ, Aristotle said, "Soul is the truth of body." We might have justification today for saying that "religion is the truth of science." Even the words of a psychologist who is a nonbeliever carries the note of a religious ecstasy:

> ...in moments of heightened self-consciousness, exultant joyous, beholding splendor afar off on the mountains, grasping at times more than an illusion of truth; for one short second, the battleground of eternities, acutely aware that he is the meeting place of permanence and change; knowing that his soul is the "truth of body" and that in self-knowledge lies his salvation and his destiny, the one thing that gives him meaning above the dumb creation of which he is the last representative to date; he, the youngest thing in the universe—and the oldest—since the forces revealed by his own physics and chemistry, his biology and psychology, and much more besides, have gone into the making of his Body-Soul.

The man of religion with his concern for the "much more beside" that science dare not approach is the custodian of the final meaning of both life and science.

With this confidence in his distinctive function in society, the pastor can accurately evaluate his mission in relation to both the tools of science and the insight of faith. He understands what the famous Christian Psychologist D. S. Waterhouse had in mind when he wrote:

> The church should be responsible for setting apart and training a ministry of healing which would have the confidence of medical men. At present every clergyman has people coming to him who should consult a physician, and ev-

ery physician has cases which are really cases for spiritual help. But sooner or later must come the day when the care of the body, of the mind and of the soul will meet together, and when the spiritual advisor, the psychologist and the medical man will cooperate in a united ministry of healing, and the body and soul God hath joined will no longer be put asunder.

Erich Fromm emphasizes that "the aim of therapy is not primarily adjustment but optimal development of a person's potentialities and the realization of his individuality." Religion is dedicated to more than adjustment. Dr. John Southerland Bonnell tells of a man released after a period of psychotherapy as healed who came to him saying, "My doctor told me I was healed and now could go on under my own steam. But that is just my trouble, I have no steam." While the conflicts of the past may be resolved and adjusted, there is always need for an adequate purpose for life to make the future inviting. The "optimal development" is another phrase for a "sense of purpose."

Religion with its desire to make people at home in the universe, brothers one of another as they are children of one Creative Spirit, is concerned with power to live. Ours is a task of teaching a maturity that can look toward the future with faith rather than fear, and toward other people with love rather than antagonism. Again Dr. Fromm says, "People believe that to love is simple but that to be loved is most difficult . . . They do not know that the real problem is not the difficulty of being loved, but the difficulty of loving; that one is loved only if one can love." Most mental illness starts in the inability of the personality to love, and the preventative work of the ministry is at the point of helping people to learn the greatest of all arts, the art of love, for love is of God, and God is love.

Dr. Charles T. Holman, who has done much useful work in this field, wrote years ago that the special resources of the pastor are the insights of religion that God is love, and that a worthy cause can make life itself worthy, and that the Christian can live in the belief that he is a potential and actual partner with God. Every pastor can in his pulpit and in his counseling room and in his own life declare the positive truths of his faith. That is a healing ministry. Then he may seek to make it his mission to raise the level of his personal competence as a worker with people, realizing that in so doing he is raising the level of his profession. For the more persons who feel that the work of preaching and pastoral care are bound together in a common cause, the more is hastened the day when the church through its worship will be making the best use of its opportunity for group therapy and where the pastor through his counseling will be doing the most effective personal work of healing. For the pastor's passion for people, when it is combined with the scientist's insight into the dynamics of human behavior and motivation, can make a combination to bring saving health to God's people.

Chapter 8

Hazards

We have been emphasizing the special privileges and opportunities that can come with parish counseling. We feel a wise use of the counseling opportunities of the parish can enrich the ministry to the parish and give rich rewards to the pastor who is able to function creatively with his people in this way.

But it would not be wise to leave the subject of parish counseling without pointing out that there are hazards to which one must be alert. Let us look at some of these briefly.

When a pastor is deeply concerned about his people there is a strong temptation to become emotionally involved with them. The pastor can take their problems as his own and suffer with them. When this happens the pastor may lose his objectivity and perspective. Then he will be less able to be helpful to those he would serve.

The professional role in working with people calls for a skill in awareness of the counselee and his feelings without an obligation to make his feelings your own. We see the analogies with every other profession. A dentist does not have to share every toothache with his patients in order to understand the hurt and the need for relieving it. A lawyer does not have to break the law in order to understand the legal plight of his client. A physician does not have to have the symptoms of disease to diagnose and prescribe for his patients. A nurse does not need to have the discomforts to sense the need of her patients for relief. Nor does the parish counselor have to have every problem of his people in order to respond to them in a wise and helpful manner. In fact, the professional is characterized by his ability to recognize the right of others to have the feelings they have without feeling that such recognition must lead to personal involvement in those feelings. The ability to remain objective is basic to the professional's role in helping to resolve problems. To the degree that the pastor becomes emotionally involved with his people he tends to reduce his effectiveness in serving them.

The pastor must protect himself against those who would take advantage of him for unworthy purposes. He must be alert to those who are emotionally starved and who seek to use him to satisfy unhealthy emotional needs. It may be that individuals in the parish have unresolved sibling rivalries at a lower level of consciousness and would seek to use a close relationship with a father figure to gain special privileges in relation to the other members of the parish. It may be that those who suffer from low self-esteem seek to bolster their feelings about themselves by demanding more time and attention from their pastor than would normally be warranted. It may be that the overdependent latch onto the pastor as a security figure and want to have him take over and manage their lives.

It may also be that the hostile and aggressive find that their pastor is a person toward whom they may safely direct their anger, and so they use his greater understanding as a license for angry acting out. Because of the many roles the pastor serves in a parish, the angry person may have many different ways for showing his feelings—anywhere from canceling his pledge to starting unhealthy rumors. In such situations the pastor must place the needs of the person over his concerns for the institution and trust the strength and security of the group to absorb and manage the unhealthy behavior of its individual members. While the pastor is highly vulnerable in his multiple parish relationships, he is wise to avoid moving toward a defensive stance which may give vent to his repressed hostility and reduce his chance of effectively counseling in the long run.

Perhaps the best protection of the parish counselor in the face of those who would abuse their relationship is a clear and assured understanding of his role and the determination to preserve it in all circumstances. His own self-assurance and his freedom from any hostile response will serve him best and preserve the form of relationship he seeks with his people.

Another hazard in parish counseling is the matter of rightly dividing one's time. In the one hundred and sixty-eight hours of the week he needs time for himself and for his own family obligations. He needs time for the organization and group life of the parish, for this can serve his basic purpose of observing his people in different contexts. Also he needs to preserve and wisely employ his priestly functions, for within this activity he can also observe his people and become sensitive to their needs, spoken and unspoken. Because his interest in people is related to a growing area of human knowledge, he wants also to preserve for himself time for study and self-development. Within this framework of multiple activities he must also leave adequate time for his constant encounter with his people. This calls for the establishing of priorities and for the wise use of his limited time.

Any parish priority list would put first those times of emergency such as illness and death. But there are other crises that call for immediate response by the pastor. A pastor would not fail to appear for a wedding just because a troubled person wanted to talk with him. The balanced approach to his many obligations makes it possible to fit many demands on his time into their proper places. Skill in this form of balance can serve the pastor well not only in his personal commitments but also in his relationship to the organization through which he functions.

Problems of confidentiality also can be a hazard for a pastor. It is clearly recognized in professional practice and in law that the statements of a parishioner to his pastor are among the most highly privileged utterances of his life. The pastor cannot under any circumstances fracture this rule of confidentiality. This, however, does not restrict his use within privileged professional channels of action that may be designed for the welfare of one of his people. Here the rule that is employed in other professional circumstances applies. A physician can consult another physician and use confidential information for the good of his patient but never for his own defense or his own amusement.

People who confess to their pastor may find immediate emotional release from their confession, but they may harbor resentment and hostility because they know the pastor knows something about them that they would prefer to have no one know. They may act out their resentment by unkind acts and words. They trusted the pastor with their secret and now they trust him with their confidence, for they are quite sure that he will not defend himself at their expense.

People who counsel with their pastor may misinterpret his willingness to be an uncritical listener. They may go to him with moral problems and, when he does not become judgmental, interpret his attitude as approval. Though the counselee may act without the restraint upon communication, the pastor must still preserve its confidentiality even though he makes his general attitude clear through other forms of communication that are open to him. But he never becomes defensive at the expense of any individual who has communicated with him in confidence.

The pastor carefully avoids any homiletic illustrations that have a resemblance to any counseling situation, for persons may be so sensitive to such likenesses that they become offended and limit further communications with their pastor. Others in the congregation may well assume that their confidences would be made public. The more sensitive and needy the person may be the more apt is he to be sensitive about his personal and private utterances.

But while there are some hazards to the role of the parish counselor, they are far outweighed by the importance of the task Not only does it bring guidance and release from stress to the people counseled, but also it gives an important dimension of meaning to the ministry of any pastor in a parish. The hazards of not fulfilling that ministry are greater than the disciplines involved in its fulfillment.

SECTION TWO:
The Parish Encounter

Chapter 9

Exploring the
Parish Encounter

The research physician speaks of his encounter with other humans professionally as clinical material. The social worker usually refers to his encounters with people as case material. The parish minister does not usually employ such terms, for his approach is more broad-based and less easily defined. Perhaps the material in these next pages should best be described as pastoral encounters.

These encounters do not fall into a set pattern. They do not attempt to cover the whole gamut of pastoral encounters. There has been a deliberate effort to leave out the more spectacular events like trying to talk the suicidally disturbed person out of his impulse to jump off the bridge. Nor is there the casual encounter that may be significant that does not go into important material related to some life circumstance.

There is no effort here to stay within the confines of verbatim material, although much of it is used where it seems useful. Rather, the effort is to show in a variety of parish encounters how conversation moves and what it feels like when it is moving. Some of the people talked to knew they were being counseled, and others probably had no clear idea that counseling was taking place. Some of the best counseling done in the parish may be in small groups. That material has been deliberately left out, for it is a whole other subject and should be considered seperately at some other time.

These following pages are not set up as representing ideal ways of engaging in the pastoral encounter in the parish. The careful reader will recognize many places where the pastor has missed opportunities and has said something that delayed or interfered with the psychological movement of the counselee. These errors may be quite as instructive as the more felicitous responses. Sometimes reference was made to religious material as would be natural for the pastor in the parish setting. At other times there seemed to be no purpose in the specifically religious focus, though in the presence of the pastor it must be considered often implicit.

Each encounter has an introduction that prepares the reader for what follows so that he may be properly oriented and may move into material that might otherwise seem unrelated. Each encounter ends with a conclusion that evaluates some of the movement with an assessment of what helped or hindered the process.

Because this encounter with actual human experiences in the parish may be a useful way for anticipating what may happen, or evaluating what has happened, it is presented as it happened, with names changed of course, and in some cases reduced to fit the limitations of space. But aside from these limitations, this is the way the parish encounter was seen through the eyes of one pastor.

Chapter 10

Sudden Infant Crib Death Syndrome

Often the pastor is called into a tragic life event with no warning or opportunity to prepare. He is expected to play several roles at once: to be a parent figure who gives emotional support, a friend who gives understanding, and a spiritual guide who works to find the spiritual resources adequate to meet the tragic events of life.

It is important in advance of such events for the pastor to get all of the insight and information he can find that might be used in such crises.

In this pastoral encounter the pastor has the advantage of a close relationship to the young couple, for he had related to them ceremonially and had visited them as a friend. Now he moved into the counselor's role strengthened by his other pastoral activities.

The pastor was in his study when the telephone rang. An excited woman said, "Nancy Schaeffer is standing in front of her house screaming as loud as she can scream. What should I do?"

The pastor said, "I'll be right over. Try to find out what the trouble is and call the police or ambulance. And stay with Nancy."

The pastor had married Nancy and Robert about three years before this day. He had visited in the home and also had baptized Bobby, who was now six months old.

When the pastor arrived at the home a police car was already there and an ambulance from the fire department. Several neighbors were standing around near the sidewalk. The pastor recognized the woman who had called him earlier and went toward her. She said, "Its Bobby. She found him dead in bed. She called the police and ambulance and fire department and doctor as fast as she could. I guess they're all in there now."

The pastor entered the door. He could see persons working with oxygen equipment and a resuscitator. Nancy, who was standing in a group of persons, finally saw her pastor and rushed toward him with arms outstretched. The pastor wrapped his arms around her and she started to sob on his shoulder. He held her for several minutes while a variety of people milled around. It was as if he were shielding Nancy from the crowd and the confusion. During all this time the pastor said nothing except her name.

Robert, the husband, who had apparently been called to come home at once without further details, came in from the office where he worked several miles away. He looked around in confusion and asked, "What are all these people doing here? Can't we get everybody out of here? Where's Nancy?"

Nancy called out, "I'm here." And when her husband came closer she said, "It's Bobby. He's dead."

Robert said, "Oh no. It can't be. He was all right this morning. What happened? Why did you leave him alone? Where is he now? Why didn't you call me sooner?"

Robert was interrupted by a detective who came up and said, "Are you the father of this child? I've got to ask you some questions. You know this is a coroner's case. Was the baby all right when you left this morning? Does your wife usually take good care of the baby? Did your wife want the baby? Are you sure your wife loved the baby?"

After gasping out a series of affirmative answers Robert asked the detective to leave him alone. He said that he wanted to stay with his wife. "Come back again later."

But the detective was insistent. He said, "This is a routine investigation. Just for the record. Just a few more simple questions. Has your wife ever been a patient in a mental institution. Is she normally a well balanced and dependable person? Have you any reason to think that your wife would abuse or neglect your baby?"

With each negative answer Robert became more exasperated with the detective's interrogation and summarily said, "Please leave me alone and get out of the house."

The detective responded, "Don't be upset, Mr. Schaeffer, this is merely routine. No offense intended. Just for the record, you know. I think I have all I need now. Just stay around so we can reach you if there is anything further. Thanks."

Robert went toward Nancy again and said, "What's this all about? Why all the questions? What did you do or what didn't you do? Somebody make sense around here."

Nancy said, "I don't know. I don't know. Oh God, if I only knew. Questions. Questions and more. And I don't know." And she came back crying on the pastor's shoulder.

In the confusion that followed, people were coming and going with or without equipment. Finally the medical examiner came up and said, "I have made my examination. We would like to have an autopsy in a case like this. Will you sign a permission form?"

Nancy burst into tears again and said, "Oh no. He is so small and helpless. They can't do that to him."

The medical examiner said, "In cases like this we have the authority to order a PM examination. Any suspicious death is a medical examiner's case. But we'd rather have your permission, of course. We get quite a few of these deaths over the years and we're trying to get the pattern. We'd like you cooperation."

Robert said, "This is all so sudden. We're confused. We want to do the right thing. I'll sign if it's necessary." Then he looked around and said, "I want to see Bobby first. Where is he?"

The nursery was empty of officials by now and the pastor followed Robert and Nancy in. There was silence. The pastor closed the door. The beautiful unmarked child lay in his crib as though sleeping. Both parents rather tentatively touched the child as if trying to grasp the frightened truth that had invaded their lives. They cried, and the pastor put his arms around them both. No words were spoken for a long time.

The medical examiner knocked, opened the door and said, "We'll probably be able to release the body this evening so you can call your own funeral director. The death certificate is on the mantle. The ambulance will bring the body to the path lab."

It was about an hour later that the pastor and the parents were sitting in the living room talking. Nancy said, "I suppose we'll have to call the grandparents. But I hate to do it. I don't know what to say. Everybody asks 'What happened?' I don't know what happened. If I knew I think it would be easier."

The pastor said, "Do you and Robert know much about sudden infant crib death syndrome? Because if you don't you should get some information right away before you have to answer too many more questions. Nothing is going to make this tragic event easy to manage, but certainly there are some things that can make it possible for you to talk with other people with more basic knowledge.

Both Nancy and Robert readily agreed that they knew nothing about SICDS, and both agreed that it would be important to try to find out as much as they could before they had to go through the inevitably painful process of calling their relatives and friends.

The pastor said that he had recently received a tape on SICDS from a tape-of-the-month service to which he belonged. He suggested that they come with him to his study where they might be able to listen to it without interruption and talk about it. Then they might be better set for all of the questions and comments that would be coming in the next few hours and days. They agreed to go with him at once. It seemed as if they were relieved to get out of the now so empty house.

Driving to his study there was little or nothing said, but there was certainly lots of thinking and feeling going on. Once in the study the pastor set up the recorder and as he did so described the tape. He said it was developed by the Center for Death Education and Research at the University of Minnesota, and all of those participating had gone through the experience of loss due to SICDS themselves. The pastor explained that there was a cutoff pedal and that if they wanted to say anything at any time to do so, for he could stop the tape instantly.

The tape explained that there is a medical mystery surrounding SICDS. Because of this lack of clear knowledge there is much conjecture and misinformation. This leads to much unintended cruelty and suspicion.

Here Nancy interjected some comments about that question, "What happened?" She said every time she heard it she felt more guilty, as if she had done something. And Robert said he was so angry at the detective who questioned him that he felt like cramming his fist down his throat. But probably he didn't know much about SICDS and had to be excused for his unintended brutality.

The tape continued to give the ancient history of SICDS with Biblical references. Then it talked about the way SICDS occurred even in hospitals and when nurses and pediatricians were present. It mentioned the occurrence of the phenomenon in the homes of physicians and specialists in the care of babies.

The tape described the medical research and the few things that had been learned amidst the large number of medically unanswered questions. Then it called for a wide program of professional and public education designed to help those who experienced loss through SICDS rather than the all too prevalent process by which injury is added to an already overwhelming form of grief, the loss of a child.

When the tape ended there was more discussion about it, and Nancy said it had helped her so much. She said, "When you don't know anything about a disease and then all of a sudden it hits you, it certainly helps to get even a little knowledge. Now when I call people and talk with them I can at least say something more than 'I don't know.'"

The pastor asked if Nancy and Robert would like a cup of hot coffee, and as they sat talking together it was as if they were trying desperately to come to terms with a shock so great that they could not comprehend it. Often the phrases like, "I still can't believe it," "It just can't be so," and "How could something like this happen to us?" were mixed with other phrases like, "I'll call my parents and you call yours," "That medical examiner didn't seem to have any feelings at all," and "What is the name of that funeral director who ushers in church some Sundays?"

A variety of practical details were talked about, and it was clear that the painful task of adjusting to a new reality was being faced. This was interspersed with tearful moments and comments that were related to deep feelings. Nancy commented to the pastor at one point, "I'm so glad when you came in this morning you didn't try to say anything. Everybody there was talking, but you seemed to know that there were no words for our feelings. And thanks for your shoulder to cry on. That was worth more than words."

When the pastor and the young parents returned to their home Nancy noticed the death certificate behind a candlestick on the mantel. She picked it up to read it and let out a gasp. "Look, it says cause of death suffocation—that isn't right, is it? I've got to get that changed. It was SICDS, wasn't it? Even the doctors don't seem to know the difference."

The pastor stayed close by the young couple until some of their friends and relatives came to stay with them. He stopped back every few hours for the next few days. He shared the funeral with the family and communicated with the secretary of the SICDS foundation in the nearby city. They sent a representative, a young nurse who had suffered a similar loss, and in their common anguish began to develop the understanding and strength needed to work through such a harrowing human experience. Instead of being devastated and divorced from each other, they found strength in each other's understanding, and grew.

While this was a specific form of counseling, it was carried on in several different settings, the home, the car, the pastor's study and through the funeral, a form of ceremonial acting out, all blended together to serve a deep emotional need. Information was provided, reassurance and comfort was given, and the multiple role of the pastor was illustrated.

Chapter 11

"The World Is an Enemy"

Persons who come to their pastor for counseling are often moved by personal crises. These may have a time element involved that makes it necessary to act rapidly and does not allow for more careful and cautious exploration of feelings. Rather it requires that direct action be taken about circumstances that are imminent. These might be referred to as short-term counseling relationships. They do not usually allow for an exposition of deep-rooted problems, although they may be quite obvious.

The following case illustrates short-term counseling. The problem is raised in its acute form. The time for coming to terms with it is set by other people and events. The pastor is obliged to work within the framework of these other people and events to help his counselee cope with the immediate problem, with the hope that growth will take place in the process. As is quite often the case with men, the problem begins in business activity and leads into the depths of his own being.

"Pastor, I'd like to talk with you if you can spare me some time," said John T. over the phone. He said the sooner the better, so I arranged to see him about 9:30 that evening after a parish meeting.

John was a quiet man who attended church regularly but never had anything to say about the services. He was a successful sales representative of a national corporation. He never gave the appearance of excessive stress or anxiety.

When John entered my study a little before nine-thirty, he was clearly upset. He moved with rather jerky motions, looked suspiciously at the chair I offered him as if it were about to be pulled from under him, took a quick glance all around the room as if it might hide some threatening object. He began to tell his story about recent events and the strange effect they had had upon him.

"I don't know whether you know it or not," he began, "but I was just promoted to district sales manager. That's a good job and I've wanted it for years. You'd think I'd be the happiest man around, but it turned out just the opposite. I'm miserable. I can't figure myself out. None of it makes sense. Helen said I should talk with you about it, so here I am."

For the time being I thought it wise to overlook the fact that his wife had engineered his visit to me, for I knew she was more the helpful type than domineering. I was quite sure that he had willingly cooperated, so that resistance was not a factor to be considered.

Out of his introductory remarks there appeared one thing that was significant, and that was his miserable state. I had not known of his advancement but did not need to mention it. His confusion about what made him miserable was important for future reference, but at this point it seemed that he was more desirous of elaborating on his misery than anything else, so I tried to help him feel comfortable in doing that. I commented, "You say you feel miserable and it doesn't make sense. How so?"

"That's the strange part of it," he continued. "It doesn't make sense. I was so thrilled when I was called into the big office. They told me the good news and everyone was as pleasant as could be. We made the plans for my takeover of the office and the setup for the next district sales meeting. Then I began to feel a bit uneasy, but I got over that in a hurry. I called home and told Helen. We went out that evening and celebrated with a special dinner. Right in the middle of it I felt uncomfortable—not sick, but uneasy."

"The routine of the changeover went along smoothly. It was a matter of moving from one office to another and getting records checked. I knew the men and the work well. The time things really hit me was at the district sales meeting. I sat in the manager's chair and had to make the presentation of plans and evaluation of sales figures. I looked around at the eyes of all those men, and I was literally scared to death. I never knew a person could suffer like that. I was shaking. I couldn't talk. Somebody said I looked sick, and I grabbed at that straw. I said I felt ill and would have to postpone the meeting for a week. Now it's creeping up on me again. I want to resign and go back to my old job, but if I did that I could never face myself again." He seemed to run out of steam and just sat for a while breathing heavily and thinking.

After a period of silence, when it seemed John was waiting for me to react to his statement, I said, "You mentioned three times that you felt uneasy or ill—almost as if it came in stages. First, you mentioned the uneasiness when you were informed of your promotion, then when you and your wife were celebrating at dinner, and finally at the sales conference. You've thought about this a good deal, I'm sure. Can you recall anything in common in these events that precipitated your reactions?"

He had made it clear that time was important, so this was a deliberate effort to move rapidly toward the center of the problem. The next meeting was coming along as a threat so great that he was thinking of resigning his new post, but he made it clear that he would be ashamed to do that. His behavior indicated a guilty feeling, but this was still only a reasonable surmise on my part. John meditated a while and then said, "Yes, the eyes." When he didn't elaborate, I followed with, "How do you mean?" "Now, don't you look at me like that. That's what I can't stand, those eyes everywhere boring into me." Then, as if he wanted to take a sharp edge off of what he had said, he laughed in an embarrassed manner.

"All right," I said. "Let's back up a little and come in more slowly. The eyes that bore into you do things to you. Can you put your finger on it?"

"I've always felt uncomfortable when people stare at me. I don't really know what it is." Then he stopped, and I felt he was wanting a nudge to move on with his thoughts and feelings.

"This uncomfortable feeling you speak of, just how does that feel?" I deliberately emphasized the feeling aspect of the matter rather than his thoughts about it.

"Well, I guess it's like this: When the big boss looked at me I felt little and on the spot; when my wife looked at me I felt afraid that I'd let her down and make her ashamed of me; and when I looked at the eyes at the sales conference, I felt all at once as if now it was twenty to one against me. I could feel what was going on behind those eyes and I just couldn't take it." His actions became quite agitated. I spoke very softly and slowly to indicate that I accepted his agitation.

"You said you could feel what was going on behind their eyes. Just how do you mean?" I asked.

"Look. I sat in those seats for twelve years. I know what those boys think. They hate my guts." He appeared to be getting angry with me, and I felt that at this point it was probably useful. I followed this up with a question that would lead him to express his anger and vent his feelings about being in the manager's role.

"How can you be so sure of that?" I queried.

"If you knew the way our company is set up, you'd know how I felt and how every one of those fellows feels. It's a real tight operation. Everybody breathes down everyone else's neck. There is only one way to get ahead and that's through a vacancy. We all sit around year after year watching the men on top retire or die, drop dead or drop out. It gets to be an obsession. On the surface you're polite and kind and you send Christmas presents and have dinner parties. But where you really live you just watch and wait. The only way up—well, you know the story. It's no way to live, but we all live that way. Except me, now. I made it—I got picked over the other twenty. Now the whole automatic process starts over again with me as the target. None of these men can get ahead until something happens to me. I have fifteen years before retirement. The thought of facing those burning eyes for fifteen minutes is too much, let alone fifteen years. Don't you get the picture at all?"

"Certainly, I can see how you feel," I replied. But it was quite obvious that he was projecting fears and feelings that he had not looked at objectively. Perhaps now was the time to do it, if he were ready. So I repeated my former question, "I asked you how you could be so sure of the feelings of the others, and what did you do? You told me how you have felt for years as if that determined how the others had to feel. Do you think that really makes sense?"

John paused a while and then answered, "You live here in your ivory tower with all your books and fancy ideas, but that's not how the world is. If you had a few days in the cutthroat, knife-in-the-back business world, you'd know what a human jungle it is. Of course, I know how things really are. This has been my life for years.

John's anger was restrained but evident. It was becoming clearer that he was not going to face his subjective emotions without some specific help. So I said, "John, I asked you if you thought your feelings really made sense. What did you do? You took some potshots at me and my ivory tower, and then went on to say with positiveness, 'This has been my life for years.' I am quite sure that is right. But a person can live in an emotional dungeon as well as in an ivory tower. Can you really determine how someone else feels by examining your own feelings?"

At this point we began an examination of how we grow to understand the feelings of others. It became clear to John that the special skill of the salesman is to manipulate and overweigh the feelings, usually sales resistance, of others. This is so much the center of attention that he makes little room for the possibility that others might have a right to different feelings. He was chosen for his new position primarily because his sales record had been better, but that probably meant that he was less responsive to the feelings of others.

Now he had been caught in a trap of his own making. His new role, and his new responsibility, would have to be characterized by a new set of feelings and attitudes. Actually he appeared to feel guilty toward the men he had won out against in the contest for district manager. When we explored this feeling, he revealed that he had always wanted to win but had never felt good about it after the victory was his. We also examined why it was that he never enjoyed winning. He assumed that everyone hated the winner, and although he wanted to win, he always lost what he wanted most by winning, the friendship and respect of those he defeated. It developed that he never played team games, had never enjoyed the contest for the contest's sake.

It was nearly midnight when we finished working through this part of his emotional background. I knew that it had been quite an ordeal for him, for he had had to peel away many of his defenses rather rapidly, and that can create anxiety. So I suggested that we meet the next evening at the same time for another session. He readily agreed and said that he felt much better though he didn't know why. He also said that he had discovered more about himself in one evening that he had ever known before.

The next evening he arrived on time and seemed to want to start talking at once. He said, "You know, this has been quite a day for me. I spent most of my time watching other people, trying to figure out what they were thinking and feeling. It is like a fascinating game, isn't it? I began to see some of the people around the office as I had never seen them before. Some of the things we talked about last night really cracked things open."

"How so?" I interjected.

"You know, a couple of those innocent little questions you asked really got to me. Like the one about knowing how other people feel, and the one about what a salesman is always trying to do to other people. You know, that's true, and I never stopped to think about it. And you know, I came up with an idea—a boss can be a friend. He doesn't have to be an enemy."

He looked at me as if he expected me to say something, so I commented, "That is quite a discovery, isn't it?"

"Yes, just that one idea makes a lot of difference." Then he went on to talk about his plans for the postponed sales meeting that was coming up the next morning. He talked about different men on the sales force as if they were people, not merely accusing eyes. He was not quite aware of his own enthusiasm about what he was going to do the next day until he made a reference to the last meeting. He said, "You know, I never knew a new point of view could make such a difference. I always thought I knew all the answers until you asked me some questions. Now I am not so sure of the answers, but it gives a new slant on things, looking for them."

Again we spent a couple of hours talking rather freely and quite objectively about business and people, and the way our own feelings can get in our way. When he left he seemed to have little or no apprehension about the next day's meeting, and acted quite intrigued by some rather simple insights into his own nature.

Like many of the counseling opportunities the parish affords, this was built around circumstantial factors. There was no time to consider his fear of death, his problems of identification or his unperceived immaturities. There was considerable stress, and some destructive emotions, but little at his age that warranted referral.

Things worked out better than would usually have been expected, because some relatively minor insights into his own nature were particularly useful to John immediately. While he was able to relieve considerable emotional stress through using these insights, he was able to learn by doing, and this learning worked two ways. It increased his insight into his own difficulty at the same time that it relieved the situational problem that came with his new employment.

John has not come back to me for any further conversation. When I meet him at church and at other functions he is always cordial but never makes any reference to the two late evening sessions we shared. As far as I know, he is functioning satisfactorily at his position, and the two intervening years should have given a fair basis for establishing his emotional equilibrium.

John's problem exemplifies the type of short-term situation where the need is for a judicious combination of an eductive and an authoritative role. Neither role, in and of itself, would have

been effective, considering the time and the nature of the problem. Yet together they made it possible to give both acceptance
and direction. And the pastor, by the very nature of his role, almost always has to admit that those who come to him expect to
be accepted, and yet they cast upon him a mantle of authority
that they expect to have exercised, whether the pastor wants it
that way or not.

Chapter 12

"Since I've Been to College I Can't Believe in Prayer"

Some of the opportunities for parish counseling come in the most unexpected settings. Part of the process emerges from pastoral accessibility. The pastor sits on a bench at a Little League team practice and has a chance to talk with parents. After the game he has a chance to engage in serious spiritual exploration with the coach of the team. None of the aspects of formal counseling exist, but the process goes on anyway.

In this encounter the pastor had a tendency to be defensive of religious points of view and was mildly manipulative, but evidently it did not offend his young friend, for the conversation kept moving. It opened the door for several more fruitful discussions before Fred returned to college in the fall.

During the summer months Fred had been acting as coach of the Little League team from the church. When he started to college Fred had some idea of going into religious work. In the fall he would be entering his junior year. While he was still quite active in the parish and the youth program, he had developed some doubts about religious work in general and the ministry in particular.

Dusk was approaching. It was becoming difficult to see the ball. Fred yelled, "Practice is over. You kids get home now. Be back here Friday at 6:30. You know we have a game Saturday. Come on now, all of you, get going. Home next stop."

The pastor had been sitting in the stands with some of the parents when Fred came over. He stood around making some casual comments until the parents had gone. Then he said, "Do you have to go now? I'd like to talk awhile."

The pastor said, "I can stand the bugs as well as you can. Sure, I can stay. I'd love to talk with you."

Fred said, "Here, use some of my bug juice. It works." They both rubbed their arms, faces, necks and ankles, then sat down again.

"What's on your mind, Fred?" the pastor asked.

"Oh, I don't know really. I've been doing lots of thinking lately. All sorts of things. I like the kids. They're a lot of fun. I like the youth program. But there are some things I have a lot of trouble believing." Then he paused, and the pastor waited and listened.

Fred continued. "There were a lot of things I always took for granted. I guess I said if everyone else believes all these things they must be all right. So I believed them too. But that doesn't work anymore. When I do my own thinking I come up with different answers."

"Like what?" the pastor interjected.

"Oh, there's lots of things. The Bible, evolution, the miracles, where you go when you're dead, and prayer. Even God." Fred talked slowly with long pauses.

"Where would you like to start exploring?" the pastor said.

"Well, take prayer, for instance. I used to believe in prayer. I prayed a lot—it made me feel good. But it doesn't seem to make sense anymore. It just isn't that kind of universe," Fred asserted.

"How do you mean, it isn't that kind of a universe?" the pastor inquired.

"Well, prayer tries to break the cause-effect chain."

"Elaborate on that, will you, Fred?"

"We learn in science that everything is built on an unbroken chain of causes that produce effects, which in turn become the causes for further effects. In chemistry you can start chain reactions. In physics the same thing is true. Even with people, if they act in a certain way there is a reason for it—some cause that makes the effect. See what I mean?"

"Yes" the pastor answered, "but what has this to do with prayer?"

"Well, you know yourself prayer is always trying to interfere with the cause-effect chain. It's asking God to intervene—to cause a miracle—to do what wouldn't be done otherwise. We pray for sick people to get well and it doesn't have anything to do with medicine. We know people pray for rain when there's a dry spell or for a sunny day when there's a picnic. You know, I just can't buy that stuff anymore. That isn't the way the universe is." Fred was getting a little excited.

"Yes, I see what you mean" the pastor said and waited.

Fred continued. "I guess what I'm trying to say is that I can't buy the kid stuff. I even tried to hold to the kid stuff for a while out of loyalty to you and my parents. But it didn't wash. I can't make myself believe what I know from science isn't true." Then after a long pause Fred looked intently at his pastor and said, "What I really want to know, I guess, is how you hold on to all that garbage. You don't really believe it, do you?"

The pastor responded, "What you're asking is how your parents and I can deny the truth. Do you think it is possible that we have raised the same questions you ask but have come up with some different answers?"

"Yes," Fred said. "I've thought of that, but I don't see how that could be. The truth is the truth, and you just can't play around with it. Cause-effect is basic. No one has a right to fool people or give them hope when it is always just a matter of natural law at work. That would be a crime against people. That would be a terrible thing to do."

"All right, Fred. Let's come in slowly on that. Just before the Wright brothers made their flight at Kitty Hawk a group of aeronautical engineers offered the scientific dictum that only lighter-than-air craft could fly and that research on heavier-than-air craft should be abandoned because it was impossible for heavier-than-air craft to fly. In June you flew home from college in a plane with several hundred other people at nearly six hundred miles an hour. The plane weighed hundreds of tons and carried hundreds of tons of cargo. What happened? How can that be explained?"

"But that's really another matter," Fred said. "Those engineers were uninformed. They didn't know about some of the other principles the Wrights were discovering. Power and motion and lift brought some other cause-effect factors into the picture. I don't see how that proves anything about prayer."

"Maybe not," the pastor conceded. "What I was trying to point out is that science also grows. New natural laws are discovered. That is the whole history of science—old laws outgrown and new ones discovered. New concepts of reality have to be taken into account constantly. The Wrights found some new laws to work with, and you shared the benefits of their willingness to disbelieve the scientific authorities of their day."

Fred argued, "But you have to admit science deals with facts and not opinions. Opinions may change, but the facts remain the same. Even scientists have to change their opinions when new facts come along."

"Yes, I agree," the pastor said. "But often the new facts are laws that have been operating a long time but have just been discovered by scientists. Could you think of prayer as a form of meaningful behavior with its own cause-effect processes at work? Could you think of any situations where prayer could make sense?"

"What are you getting at?" Fred queried.

"I've been doing some reading lately in psychosomatic research. The basic premise now seems to be that disease is a form of organic behavior. If the meaning of the behavior is discovered it throws light not only on the origin of the disease but also on how to treat it. Often it seems that the attitude of mind of the person shows up in the nature of the disease. Does it seem possible to you that prayer might have something to do with a person's attitude of mind?"

"You mean that prayer is like talking to yourself?" Fred asked. "Then it would be just like self-hypnosis, a kind of psychological tool to fool one's self."

"Or better, it might be a way of looking at life that could change things for the better—purify one's emotions and gain needed perspective. Recently I read that it is dangerous to sit down to eat a heavy meal when angry. Prayer might be used to flush the anger out of the system and put some different emotions in its place. Maybe it would be valid to pray before a meal just to ensure a better digestion. Does that make any sense to you, Fred?" the pastor asked.

"Sure, but that's not what I've been driving at. I can see that form of self-hypnosis. But you can't hypnotize the universe. That's what I'm talking about."

"Even hypnosis seems to have laws at work. Probably most people are at work making powerful suggestions to themselves all the time. These suggestions may be clues to larger systems of law that may be at work in the universe for either good or ill. But prayer seeks to find the meanings for life that can produce good fruits in living," the pastor suggested.

"Oh that's the old positive-thinking line. Look at the world through rosy glasses and it will all look better. I don't go much for that."

"Neither do I, if you reduce it to the level of manipulation. But if you lift it to discovery of valid principles for living, it can be quite different. But you spoke of manipulating the universe, and that is another matter for discovery. It may be that the universe is different from what we have thought. The president of MIT said it appears now that the universe is more like a great thought than like a great thing. Physicists speak of reality in energy terms, and recent studies show that the mind is an energy creating organism. Research at the Menninger Clinic in biofeedback shows that skillfully directed thought processes can prevent migraine headaches. We are getting into areas where a whole new range of cause-effect processes are being explored. The type of mental activity involved in prayer, then, is seen in a new light."

"Now you're changing the idea of prayer. That's not the way
we were taught to think about it. That is not asking for things,"
Fred challenged.

"You're right. Too often in church and church school we've
given a trivial concept of prayer as pleading, begging, trying to
manipulate the universe emotionally. I had to go through a lot of
growth to get rid of that idea. But now I think of prayer as a discipline, an attitude and a process of self-discovery in myself and
in relation to others and the larger focus of life in the structure
of the universe. I find this idea of prayer much more challenging. It demands more and it produces more. Like everything else
our attitude toward prayer and meditation grows," the pastor
added.

"I'm glad I talked with you about this. I had the feeling there
might be more to this. I didn't think you'd really buy the garbage. Do you have the books on this so I could follow it up some
more? Then maybe we could talk some more when there aren't
so many bugs around."

"Anytime. Stop by my study and we can explore some books
on meditation, prayer and spiritual disciplines. I find this a very
challenging subject. Lots of young people are going into meditation in depth. Much is happening that would interest you, I am
sure. Glad we had a chance to talk about some of it."

"Yeah, thanks. I'll stop by. Night." And Fred took off.

In looking back at this conversation it is clear that certain
things that should have been explored were omitted. Fred was
probably dealing with important feelings, and he gave several
clues to this. But the pastor tended to deal with the whole matter
more at the intellectual level and through ideas rather than feelings. This is a common temptation of pastors, and it is wise to be
on guard against this tendency.

Chapter 13

"If I Don't Get Some Sleep I'll Go Crazy"

Sometimes people do not bother to call in advance but burst in on the pastor. Men especially may do this on Saturdays, for it is often their only free day, so it is wise for the pastor to allow some elasticity in his schedule for this day.

This pastoral encounter, because of the close relationship the pastor had with the man, was a little difficult to get into. The pastor wanted to be the friend but felt he should not overplay the friendship. This led to some stiffness at the beginning and a couple of leads that could certainly have been improved on.

Because this man was well trained and used psychological insight in his work, it seemed that after the direction of the encounter was established the counselee took it away, and psychological movement was rapid. Also, because of the emergency nature of the problem, plenty of time was given to a specific plan of action. Sometimes this type of prescription sets up a counter-direction for emotional energy that is important for the resolution of the problem.

Oliver Lipscomb was a professional investigator, connected for many years with the nation's most prestigious bureau of investigation. He usually acted with assurance, had no hesitation in confronting difficult problems and appeared to have a well-balanced and competent approach to life.

Oliver was an active and useful member of the parish and a friend of the pastor, with whom he had worked on many parish projects over a number of years.

So it was quite out of character for him to respond with acute anxiety and obvious difficulty in meeting life events.

It was on a Saturday morning that he appeared, unannounced, at the pastor's study. His eyes were red and had a hollow look that suggested haunting experience. Oliver accepted an invitation to come in and be seated. He slumped into a chair and said, "I've got to have some help."

The pastor responded, "How do you mean?"

"If I don't get some sleep, I'm going to go crazy."

"So something's bothering you. Do you want to tell me about it?"

"I wish I could," Oliver said, "but I don't really know what is the matter. I stopped at the bureau's medical office and they checked me out. Nothing the matter with me physically. Gave me some pills—sleeping pills, I guess. They didn't do any good. This thing's building up, and if I can't get a good night's sleep soon I think I'm headed for a breakdown of some kind. They think I'm working too hard and I should ease up for a while, but I know that isn't it, for I worked harder lots of times and never felt like this."

After a pause the pastor said, "Why don't you tell how your sleeplessness started and how it affects you?"

"Oh, it's been coming on for six weeks or a couple of months now. I didn't really notice at first, I guess. I just stayed up later and later and puttered around doing things or watching the late news and old movies. Nothing serious at first. But the last couple of weeks it's been getting worse. Now I get ready for bed but can't make myself get into the bed. I pace back and forth—for hours sometimes. It seems like some force is holding me away from the bed. I think I'm going to get in but then something takes hold of me and I start pacing again. This goes on for hours until I'm so exhausted I fall on the bed. Sometimes it's four or five o'clock. That's no time to get to bed when I have to catch the 7:52 train. This morning about four I finally sat on the edge of the bed and cried like a baby. Betty tried to calm me, but it just made things worse. She said I had to come see you this morning, so here I am."

The pastor said nothing and waited while Oliver looked out the window.

"When something's the matter and you don't know what it is," Oliver continued, "it's worse than if you did. It makes you feel so helpless. I feel so angry at myself. Always before I could handle things. Real bad things. Now this. It makes no sense at all. You're supposed to know about people's insides. What do you make of all this?"

"Well, people's insides are interesting and complicated and sometimes quite baffling. That's why we have to do some exploring. Has there been anything at work that has gotten to you?"

"No. I have just been carrying routine cases lately. Mostly for job clearances. Nothing at all to bother me. In fact, a good juicy case right now would be a welcome change."

"Has there been anything else you can think of that happened in the last few months that would upset you?" the pastor asked.

"That is what makes it so stupid, the whole bit. There is nothing to cause it, and how can you have an effect without a cause?" Oliver continued.

"Cause-effect. They always go together. But sometimes the cause is obscure. That's when we have to explore more carefully. It's bound to be there, but sometimes it's quite a job to get at it. You don't mind if we explore more deeply, do you?" the pastor asked.

"Of course not. That's why I came. I'm getting desperate."

"All right," said the pastor. "If I remember right your mother died not long ago. You went down to Tennessee for the service. I remember talking with you about it at the time."

"Yes, that's right. But that didn't really bother me. You know, she was old, her mind was gone and it was a blessing. She'd been in a nursing home for six years. We all expected it, and so I can't see how that would explain things. She hadn't been herself for years. It was no tragedy. In fact, we were all so relieved that she was out of her misery that we didn't shed a tear."

"Let's explore this some more, if you don't mind. Let's go back a bit. What is the first thing you can recall about your mother. What is your earliest memory of her?"

Oliver thought for quite a while before he said, "I think it was saying my prayers at night. She'd get us ready for bed, and then she'd sit on the bed and I'd kneel down at her knees and say my prayers, and then she always gave me a hug and kiss and tucked me in. Yes, I think that's the earliest recollection I have of her."

"Tell me all you can remember about your thoughts and feelings about your early prayer."

"Oh, I don't think there is much to tell. It must have been important for me to remember it. But it was just one of those times when love was expressed and I guess it made me feel good. But that's all. I wouldn't make a big thing out of it."

"What was the prayer you said? Can you remember?" asked the pastor.

"Oh, sure. It was the prayer all kids said. You know the one: 'Now I lay me . . .' "

"How did that prayer end, Oliver?"

"You know, 'if I should die before I wake, I pray the Lord my soul to take.' " Then Oliver went back and repeated the whole prayer slowly and with considerable meaning.

"When did you stop saying that prayer?" asked the pastor.

"You know, I never really did. Always when I go to bed I say that prayer my mother taught me, and then I add the Lord's Prayer. And that's it."

The pastor tried hard to keep from showing his amazement that this layman who had heard many sermons on the meaning and value of prayer should still employ this childish approach to prayer, but this was not the time for lessons on prayer. Something deeper was involved.

So the pastor asked, "Do you see any cause-effect process at work here—I mean your prayer, your mother's death and your inability to go to bed?"

Oliver sat thinking for quite a while. Then he said, "You know, you might just have something there. You know, in our work we have to take courses in psychology and behavior. I could see connections with other people, but me—well, I don't usually apply it to myself . . . "

The pastor continued to listen as Oliver thought in silence.

Then Oliver spoke up again: "Do you think my mother could have been some kind of a security blanket for me? Do you think I kept saying that prayer all my life because I wanted to feel my mother close by and knew that she would hug and kiss me? Yes, I think we've got something here. Would you believe it? You know, after she died I couldn't pray anymore. I never thought about it. I just didn't feel like it, I guess. What do you make of that?"

The pastor remained silent, for it seemed Oliver was asking the question of himself.

Oliver continued, "You know, we've learned that what happens to kids affects them for a long time. But I never thought much about it with myself. You know what? When she died I lost something. Even when she was sick I knew she was there. I could keep her alive in my mind. But when she died, something happened. It wasn't that I didn't want to pray. Somehow or other it just didn't seem right. And I kept putting it off—puttering around or watching TV. Maybe I didn't want to admit that my mother was really dead." He paused quite a while and then continued: "Do you think that's it?"

"Well," the pastor said, "I think you're getting close to something that may be important. How do you feel about it?"

Oliver again sat for a long time looking out the window. "Well, let me restate it. So I hold on to my mother all through the years. I use the child's prayer to do it. Then when she dies the whole thing falls apart. But I can't admit it to myself, so I keep on denying it and this whole inner conflict shows up in the sleep bit. Is that the way it looks to you?"

"Could be," the pastor said. "But it is more important how it feels to you than how it looks to me."

Again Oliver thought a while and finally said, "You know, there's something else. You've spoken about prayer many times and it never seemed to touch me. You always seemed to think of it so differently. I always had the feeling that it was simple, personal, you know, very real. You always made it seem different. I guess that's why I always turned you off when you talked about the discipline of prayer and the skills of the spiritual life. It didn't make sense to me. All you had to do was kneel down by the bed and everything was taken care of. That's pretty childish, isn't it?"

Again Oliver thought a long while and then said, "You know, some of this begins to fit together and make sense. This cause-effect thing—and the sleep bit. But I don't see how it's going to help me any. So I know I've lost my security blanket. What am I going to do about it? How am I going to get a good night's sleep?"

"You're right. We have a lot more to do. But we've been working at this now for an hour and a half, and we've made some real progress. I think you'll notice a difference tonight. Maybe we can make some suggestions for the time being, and then I would like to see you Saturday mornings for a while so we can continue to work on this. I think one of the things we can do, and you can start working on this tonight, is to project a cosmic dimension to this need you feel for the mothering."

Oliver interrupted: "I don't get that. A cosmic dimension for mothering? What do you mean?"

"It seems that we have to build a new foundation for security. Something that can make you feel safe when you go to bed at night. Something like this—try it tonight and then we can check on how it works. I think it's the fourth Psalm; David is being pursued and he can't keep watch all night, so he found the safest place he could, stretched out, relaxed and said, 'I will both lay me down in peace and sleep, for Thou only, O Lord, makest me to dwell in safety.' "

"But how do you relax? I get so tense I think something will snap in my head," Oliver said.

The pastor said: "Tension seems to feed on tension. But the same mental and emotional mechanisms can be used in reverse.

You can use your mind to relax your muscles. You can practice it now. Toes, finger, feet, hands; shake the tense muscles loose and keep on going through the body. Let each muscle system be the focus of your carefully directed thought. Give special attention to your lower jaw, your neck and your diaphragm. And when you get the tension out of your body then work at your feelings, the things that bother you. Shake them loose. And then get your mind working for you to keep your thought well directed. Hold a calm and peaceful picture. Repeat the phrase I mentioned."

When it seemed Oliver was comfortable with these ideas the pastor continued.

"In our next times together we want to explore the ways of prayer that can be helpful to you as an adult. We want to think of the spiritual nature of the universe so that death is not so threatening a separation. We want to come to the place where you discover a whole new set of mothering forces in life that can meet your needs now as your prayers with your mother did when you were a child. How do you feel now?"

"You know, I feel as if a weight had been lifted. When I came in I was really scared. I thought I was losing my grip. Now I can see some reasons for what has been happening. I feel better. Maybe I'll make it."

"Oh, you'll do better than just make it. Tomorrow after church I want you to tell me what a good sleep you had last night. And then we'll keep working at this. This could all be an important growth experience in your life."

"You know, I think you're right. I feel things happening already. Thanks a lot. See you tomorrow."

Here we had a grief reaction that was obscured by other manifestations and their interpretation. But a man with considerable intelligence was able to start putting things together so that his grief was a source of growth. During eight more sessions we explored the adult skills of prayer and the spiritual philosophy of life and death so that the symptoms of distress were not only eliminated but the ways of coping with life in more mature terms were explored. After the first session, there was a sound night's sleep, and the sleeping problem did not appear to recur. Three years after the counseling, there had been no recurrence.

Chapter 14

"How Could a Good God Let Things Like This Happen?"

Often people come to the pastor with what appear to be pure-ly theological questions. Often, however, they are but a point of approach to the pastor to get at a problem with deep emotional strata. Sometimes the pastor is caught off guard and tends to assess the communication as a quest for theological informa-tion. This is a safe ground for him, for he knows more formal theology than most of his parishioners. So he must make a spe-cial effort to read between the lines and try to detect the real emotional problem to which the theological question is the pre-lude. The following encounter illustrates this type of approach to a pastor.

The pastor was calling in the home of one of his members. He knew the family was going through a crisis, for the young son, of whom the Warrens were justifiably proud, was in the hospital recuperating from surgery to remove a leg in order to control a malignancy.

After the initial pleasantries the pastor asked, "What's the latest word from the medical center?"

"Oh, Jerry seems to be in good spirits. We talk with him every evening on the phone. We're flying down Friday night to spend the weekend with him." There was a long pause, and finally Jerry's mother continued, "I think he's doing better than we are. Most of the time I'm just seething inside."

"Yes, I know. This is a terrible thing for you to have to take," the pastor said.

"That seems to be the trouble. I can't take it," said Mrs. Warren. "It is so hard to make any sense out of it. A young fellow, just twenty-two—and now this."

"You said you were seething inside and can't take it. How do you mean?"

"Well, it's so unjust. That's what I mean. So young, and now a cripple for life. And he loved football so much. They were even thinking of him as all-league quarterback. Everyone admires him so and he has such good character. So many young people now are drifters and no-goods. But nothing happens to them. But Jerry, so fine and good, I don't see how a good God could let things like that happen."

The pastor's first impulse here was to give a theological answer and try to defend God. Then he reassessed Mrs. Warren's comments and felt they were more emotional than theological; he tried to decide what would be a useful response. He finally settled for these words that he felt might make it possible for Mrs. Warren to pour out more of her feelings: "It does seem unjust, doesn't it?"

"Well, I've lived quite a long time, longer than you. I've seen lots of things happen. I hope I'm not bitter, but it seems to me that there's lots of injustice in this world. It seems as if the good are always suffering and the evil get away with murder."

"You say you hope you are not bitter," the pastor commented, trying to stay close to her feelings.

"Well, I know as a Christian I shouldn't be bitter. But it's hard not to be. You know all this stuff about trust in God and vengeance is mine, says God. It's good for those who believe it, but life seems to work the other way for me."

"You speak of vengeance, Mrs. Warren," the pastor said. "Does it seem to you that punishment is involved?"

"Well, I don't know how else you can look at it. If God is all-powerful and controls all things, He must have a hand in it somewhere."

The pastor responded, "Yes, if God is all-powerful that is one thing. But what if there are some limits on God's power?"

"It's funny to hear a preacher talk like that. You're the ones always talking about what God can do, and I never hear you say anything about what He can't do."

The pastor was trying hard not to get distracted by some of this hostility showing through, because he assumed it might divert him into a theological discussion, but he also realized it might be good for Mrs. Warren to vent some of the anger she was feeling. He said, "Some of us preachers do emphasize the power of God, but maybe we don't give enough time to exploring God's self-imposed limitations."

"That's a new one on me. God's self-imposed limitations. You must be kidding."

"No, I'm not," the pastor said. "If God expects men to be moral He must give them freedom to do wrong. When men use their freedom of choice they can do things that are contrary to God's will and purpose. Do you think.it is God's will for people to kill each other, destroy the beauty of the earth, commit crimes of all kinds?"

"I don't get it. You think Jerry committed some crime and so God is punishing him by having his leg cut off?"

"Not exactly. There may be other ways of limiting God's will. Ignorance—doctors don't know enough yet to control cancer. If men are free to do research they are also free to come up with wrong answers. Oh, we make progress, but in our fight against ignorance we have a long way to go," the pastor said.

The pastor realized he was getting theological, and he wanted to stay closer to Mrs. Warren's distressed feelings. So he decided to back up and give her a chance to pour out some more of the feelings she had expressed earlier. So he said: "Tragic things can happen without having to blame anyone. You can still feel just as upset even if you don't have anyone to blame. If you love someone and they are injured you feel the injury."

"You sure do, Mrs. Warren agreed. "The night after Jerry's operation I couldn't sleep all night. My leg ached so I couldn't stop it. Now how do you figure that? It was his leg they took off, but it was my leg that ached."

"Feelings are amazing things the way they work," the pastor said. "When you love someone you suffer with him."

"Yes, and when you love someone you feel so helpless," she mused.

"How do you mean that?"

"Maybe that's why my leg ached. I'd rather have it be my leg than his. I could get along better without it than he can. My legs are getting gimpy anyway. I guess that's where the injustice comes in. Why him and not me, when I'd make out better? There's something wrong in the whole setup."

The pastor realized that if he tried to defend the cosmic setup he would be going theological again. He wanted to stay with Mrs. Warren's feelings. So he said: "You feel there's something wrong with the whole setup. I'm not sure I understand your feeling."

Mrs. Warren seemed a bit confused. She thought awhile. Then she said, "I'm not sure I know what I mean. When I think of Jerry I want to cry. I want to do something to change things. I want to step in and say this is no way to have things happen. That's why I feel so helpless. I can't do any of the things I want to do."

"Yes, you love like a mother and you suffer like a mother," the pastor commented.

"That's the worst part of it. I'm so wrapped up in him. I think it's worse on me than it is on him. He jokes about it and says, 'Will they only be surprised when they tackle a plastic leg and it comes off in their hands,' but he knows he'll never play again. I suppose he's young and can take things as they come. But I want to fight back, and yet who can I fight?"

"That helpless feeling . . . It's harder to handle than if you could really fight something. That helpless feeling . . . It goes with parental love doesn't it?" The pastor picked up her mood.

"You're right. The worst part of it," she mused. "But you

wouldn't want to stop loving him just to make it easier on yourself. You wouldn't do that."

"Don't be foolish. That wouldn't work. You don't turn love on and off like that. You aren't serious?"

"I'm serious when I point out that love and suffering often go together. But as you say, you can't run away from love. You can't turn it on and off just to suit your own comfort." The pastor watched and waited.

After a while Mrs. Warren said: "I think I see what you're getting at. I'm suffering along with Jerry because I love him so much and I'm not going to stop loving him so I will probably just have to go on suffering. . . . Is that it?"

"That's partly it. But I think there are different kinds of suffering. Some suffering makes us angry and bitter, and we want to fight back. Some suffering makes us more tender and loving and understanding. Maybe Jerry needs someone to understand how much he is suffering underneath his humor and brave spirits." The pastor wondered if he had moved too fast and too far with that response.

Mrs Warren stared at the pastor and bit her lip as if she were trying to control some deep feelings. She then said, "You don't want me to go down there and crack up in front of him, do you?"

The pastor was uncertain about this response and how to interpret it. Was she working on something he didn't sense, or was she trying to change the direction of the conversation. So he asked, "How do you mean?"

"You know well enough what I mean. You practically came right out and said it. And it's true. I've been so selfish about my own suffering that I haven't thought much about what's going on inside of Jerry. I've been so wrapped up in my own feelings that I couldn't care less whether anyone else has any feelings at all. And you said it just like it is." And she started to cry.

After quite a spell of sobbing she quieted down and said, "I have dreaded so much going down there this week. I was so mixed up. I wanted to see him and I couldn't bear to see him. But now I think I know why. It was me I was worrying about. If I go down there concerned about him and his feelings, maybe I can do him some good. Maybe I can help him feel his feelings like you've helped me to feel my real feelings."

This had all moved faster than the pastor had thought it could. But he was relieved that she had given a constructive interpretation to what he had tried to say. He knew she had needed someone to help her understand why she had been so angry. So the pastor said, "As his mother, as one very close to him, as one who loves him in a special way, I'm sure you will help him cope with his deep suffering."

As the pastor stood up to leave, Mrs. Warren said: "Oh, I'm so glad you came by today. I was feeling terrible, and it was all part of my selfish suffering. I think I can see what you mean about unselfish suffering. If I help Jerry with his suffering maybe I won't notice my own so much. Is that what you mean?"

That was more than he had meant, and so the pastor said, "I think you've put it very well. Be sure to give Jerry our best and tell him he is a part of our prayerful thought often."

Here was one of those encounters where the human suffering was intense. Almost without realizing it the pastor's presence had become a focal point for some of the deep anger that is so often a part of suffering. Not so much by what he said but by his being there, he had given this distressed woman a chance to pour out her anger and shed her tears where they were accepted as a part of her suffering. Just the comments about suffering had seemed to be all that she needed to let it come boiling over. When she had cried out some of her feelings her perspective on her role as a mother seemed to be clarified. Then she was able to confront a difficult visit to the hospital with a sense of purpose that might do both her and her son useful service in growing through a crisis that involved them both. If the pastor had become involved in a discussion of God and the sin of bitterness, the feelings would probably have been blocked off or diverted. As it was, in spite of some clumsy responses, by staying close to the feelings, something useful seemed to have emerged from the pastoral encounter.

Chapter 15

Parish Conflicts

One of the distressing situations that comes with counseling in the parish context is the problem of failure. One cannot work with people without having circumstances develop where there is sharp disagreement. In order to protect the standards the pastor sets in his work with people, he must be willing to say and do those things that produce violent reactions, not because he wants it that way, but because to do otherwise would mean that he has compromised where compromise was not possible.

In working with people who become angered because the pastor does not conform to their wishes or does not serve their purposes, he must be prepared for reverberations that would not ordinarily come from counseling in the clinical setting. The pastor cannot isolate people from the whole context of church life, nor can he insulate himself from the reaction of unfavorable counseling relationships that touch the rest of parish activity. He is doubly vulnerable because in most situations he cannot defend himself with betraying confidence, and he cannot keep people from showing their anger in whatever ways they choose within the life of the parish.

In the following case the responsibility of the pastor was quite clear. His hope was that all parties involved might see this responsibility and act accordingly. This was not the way things turned out. He failed to be effective in ameliorating the anger of the parents involved. It may be that he served a useful purpose in giving them a safe direction for venting the anger and hostility that might have caused serious reactions if it had been internalized. However, that was not the primary goal of the counseling, and the failure to achieve the goal was a costly one in terms of the parish.

The son of a prominent family in the parish was married a few months before he went overseas with the air force. He was shot down and captured. He evidently endured serious physical injury in addition to long months of "brainwashing." When he was released, he was returned to a hospital in the United States. After a period of psychiatric treatment, he was released with the understanding that his family would be responsible for continued treatment at an outpatient clinic of the Veterans Administration. His treatment continued for some time. The pastor was aware of the condition because he had counseled the veteran's wife about the intolerable condition that she had experienced with his return. He was a completely different person, remote, inconsiderate and irresponsible. He would be away from home and unaccounted for for long periods of time. When he returned home he was abusive and irritable and complained of pains in his head. Through the psychiatrist at the VA clinic, the pastor was given a diagnosis and prognosis that was pessimistic. The physician said that the veteran had suffered severe brain damage and that there was little likelihood that he would ever be able to function normally. He had been declared totally disabled and was receiving support from the government sufficient to maintain him and his family. This was the general state of affairs when the first of a series of episodes occurred.

In response to the doorbell, I admitted a man and his seventeen-year-old daughter. He apologized for coming without an appointment but said something had developed that he felt needed immediate attention and he wanted my help. He said, "My daughter, Alice, is determined to marry a young man she has known less than a month. We feel she knows little or nothing about him. We have invited him to the house and he will not come. She says that if we do not give our consent to marry, she will run away and lie about her age. Things have become intolerable and we decided to come right over here and talk with you."

I said enough to make them feel they were welcome to come when they felt it desirable, and that I would try to help them think through their problem. Then I looked at Alice, a warmhearted young woman I had come to know quite well through the youth group in the parish, and suggested that she might want to say something.

She said, "My parents think they can run my life, and they keep on telling me what I can and cannot do just like I was a little kid. I've met a fellow who is very important to me. We are deeply in love. He was a hero in the war and was wounded. He needs love and care and I can give it to him. He needs it more than anything else right now. He has a good income so we would have nothing to worry about. When I told my parents about it you would have thought I was going to rob a bank or something. They were just impossible. I got angry and they got angry and that is when we decided to come over here. Can't you get them to see that I am old enough to know my own mind and I have a right to do the things that are important?"

From the description given I surmised that the young man in question might well be the veteran who was causing his wife so much trouble, for he was the only one I knew who fitted the description. If that were so, it would have great importance in anything further that was said and done. So I said, "Would you want to tell me anything more about your friend? Is he someone I know?"

Alice continued, "No, you don't know him. I asked him about coming to talk with you about our wedding, but he didn't want to. Said he just wanted to get married quietly by a chaplain he knew in the air force. His name is Allan Munson."

I had married Allan Munson and therefore I knew why he did not want to talk with me about his marriage, past, present or future. My main concern now was to help this girl accept some facts that she would have to face sooner or later, and do it in a way that would not be permanently damaging. Her father seemed to sense the impending revelation and wisely remained quiet.

I said, "That's strange, Alice. I knew Allan quite well. Perhaps he didn't have occasion to mention it. Tell me, Alice, how much has Allan told you about his injuries in Vietnam?"

"Oh, quite a bit. He talks about the war a lot. He was badly hurt. That's how he gets his money—from the government, you know. He is a disabled veteran, but you wouldn't know it to see him. He looks perfectly healthy," she said.

"Doesn't it seem strange to you that he would be pensioned if he were perfectly healthy? Did he mention the type of treatment he has been receiving and is supposed to be getting now?" I felt it was better to be quite directive now, for if things went much further she might be subjected to a brutally painful circumstance with no one around to ease the blow for her.

She answered, quite confidently, "Oh, I asked him about that, and he said it was internal injuries. He was to go to the hospital regularly for checkups, but it doesn't mean anything. It's just routine, at least that's what he says."

The last phrase was the first indication that she might be questioning anything he had said. She had ignored my statement that I knew Allan quite well. "You have probably observed his speech and behavior quite closely," I said. "Have you noticed anything that seemed unusual to you?"

"Oh, yes. He's the most absentminded person I ever met. He'll be talking and stop right in the middle of a sentence, and when I ask him what he was saying, he seems to come back from a long way off. He says it's the war. If I'd gone through what he has it would be the same. And sometimes he is very edgy. He gets upset easy. But that's the war, too," she added defensively.

"Yes, I think you are right," I interjected. "He was quite severely injured, and it has had serious effects. One of the tragic results of war is that people are sometimes injured in ways that don't show in their bodies, but show in their behavior, in the way they think and act."

Alice looked at her father quickly and then back at me, as if she had heard something like that before but was now thinking of it in a different perspective. I continued: "Sometimes the behavior shows in relation to other people. It could even show toward you, as you mentioned with the edginess. Sometimes persons with injuries like Allan's can't think clearly, and they need special help. They know they need help, but sometimes they seek it from people who can't give what they really need. I am sure you want to help Allan and your desire is commendable. But the doctors feel that he needs a very specialized kind of treatment."

"You mean Allan is a mental case?" Alice blurted out.

"Alice, the doctors in the air force felt his injuries were quite severe and involved brain tissue. And that shows up in a number of ways. He needs special consideration because he is not able to act responsibly much of the time."

"Then he *is* a mental case. Then he really shouldn't get married." She said this as if she were trying to take hold of an idea that was just out of reach.

I had been wondering about bringing in the information about his marriage. I wanted to do it in such a way that it would be an illustration of his ailment rather than a revelation of his duplicity, and it seemed this was the time to do it. So I continued with her last idea, trying to elaborate on it and at the same time do it protectively. "Yes, Alice, I think you are right that he shouldn't marry you. You see, in his present mental state he is not able to understand the meaning and obligation of marriage. That is probably why he doesn't understand that he is not eligible for marriage. He seems to be incapable of fulfilling the obligations of the marriage he contracted before he was so severely injured in the war."

Alice darted across the room and flung herself into her father's arms and sobbed disconsolately. He comforted her, and after a while she turned toward me and said, "Oh, what a terri-

ble thing. He is such a fine person to be so hurt inside. Oh, I
don't know what to do now. I don't know what to say to him. I
don't want to hurt him anymore. What can I do now?"

I suggested that Alice and her father and mother might want
to talk the whole matter over together and try to decide what
would be the best thing to do. I added that if I could be of any
help I would be willing to try.

Nothing more was heard of the matter until four days later,
when Allan Munson's father called in an indignant mood and
said he was coming to the church office and would like to meet
me there as soon as possible. I arranged a time an hour later,
and Mr. and Mrs. Munson arrived on schedule.

Mr. Munson was a successful businessman, blustery, super-
patriotic and convinced that the direct approach was always
best, especially if he were in the position to apply enough power.
He wasted no time in pleasantries and went directly to the subject. He said, "Of all the lowdown things I've ever heard of, what
you have done to Allan is the lowest. To kick a poor helpless boy
when he is down. To turn him against his friends. To tell people
he is crazy just because he sacrificed himself to protect you and
your kind. You don't deserve the sacrifice he made. You're not
worth it. You're the worst kind of hypocrite, pretending to be so
wise and helpful when all you can do is knife a poor injured hero
in the back. You're not going to get away with this, I'm telling
you."

Mrs. Munson was the opposite of her husband, quiet and
conciliatory, but all she was able to do was sit to one side and
wipe her eyes.

With the head of steam Mr. Munson was carrying, it was
quite clear that the logical approach was not apt to work. So I
made it easy for him to continue to vent his feelings. I said, "I
can see you are quite worked up about this matter. I wonder if
you have all the facts."

"Fact, facts," he exploded. "Who needs facts? Alice calls up
and says she has decided not to see Allan anymore. She says she
had a talk with you and you said he was a mental case. So who
needs facts? What happened is all the facts I need. I never in my
born days heard of anything lower. I don't know what could

have possessed you to do a thing like that to Allan after all he has done for you and lots of others who don't deserve it." He went on to detail other pastoral inadequacies that had come to his attention, social, personal and political. After a while his anger seemed spent and he ran down.

"Mr. Munson," I began. "I am deeply distressed about the injuries Allan received in Vietnam, and I know how distressing it must be to you. But let's get this straight. I have responsibilities I must respect. Alice came to me talking about marriage. You know as well as I do that Allan is already married. In the best way I knew how I tried to help Alice see what the circumstances were. There wasn't anything else I could do without being untrue to the marriage I had already performed for Allan. I think when you look at this from all angles you will see that what I did was necessary even though it was difficult and unpleasant to do."

"You'll find out what I think soon enough," Mr. Munson continued. "You know Allan didn't mean anything by what he said. He wouldn't hurt the girl. He just needed a friend and that was all there was to it. To make a big thing of it is just a lot of preacher meddling. If you'd left things alone, he would have handled it all right. And you are not going to get away with it. You'll hear plenty about this before I'm through with it. My wife and I are going to leave this church. But before we do everyone is going to know why. I've given plenty to this church, but I'm canceling my pledge to the church, the building fund and the Mission Crusade. You'll never get another red cent out of me after what you've done."

"You've made yourself quite clear, Mr. Munson," I said. "I respect your right to do what you think is right and necessary. If you tell the truth about what has happened, I can assure you that would be just fine with me. If you don't, that will be a matter for your own conscience."

"You're a good one to talk about truth and conscience. You who would destroy a poor boy before his friends. You'll find out what I'll say and it will be on you conscience, not mine." With that he yanked at Mrs. Munson and the two of them went out the door with an unnecessary slam.

I knew that the burden of Allan's injuries and the consequent impossible behavior had rested heavily on his parents. There had been a number of episodes where he had been in trouble with the police and others, and always his disabled veteran status had gotten him out. But this time the circumstances were different. I was not a policeman or a court. In effect, I was an employee who could be punished to the full extent of the accumulated wrath that had grown with the mental state of their son, so difficult to explain or tolerate.

In accepting the wrath of the parents I had given them a chance to express feelings that had probably not been expressed before. In assailing me they seemed to gain a satisfaction that had been denied them in other contexts. I had tried to make my position clear but beyond that had asked no consideration and had made no apology for doing what seemed necessary under the circumstances.

For two or three months the Munson matter was a major concern in the parish. At various committee meetings and board sessions letters of resignation and withdrawal were read into the minutes. Unless someone asked, no comment was made. When some comment was asked for, I merely said, "This involves matters of pastoral confidence which I feel cannot be divulged and so I will have to let the matter rest." The financial secretary tried to get a more explicit statement in private. He said, "We can't afford to lose pledges like the Munson's. What did you ever do to get him so burned up? Can't you do something to straighten things out?" Here again the matter was allowed to rest on the sacredness of the pastoral confidence.

With time the matter quieted down. Two years later Allan was still in treatment, Alice was in college, Alice's parents were active participants, and the Munsons, while not yet active, were beginning to show signs of interest in some of the group activities of the parish.

Looking back on it from a more objective position, the pastor can think of a number of things that he could have done more wisely. He could have called the Munsons in for a session to acquaint them with what had happened. He could have followed a more conciliatory approach to the Munsons in the months following the unfortunate episodes. But in the fast-breaking events of human life in the parish setting, things are bound to happen that carry emotional charges that cannot be easily managed. It is a part of the ministry to people in that unique setting where the pastor is a counselor and a servant, a spiritual guide and an agent of an institution.

Chapter 16

Abnormal Reactions to the Lord's Supper

Because of his right of privileged access to the homes of his parishioners, the pastor is often able to move toward the center of severe problems. When these human circumstances would be carefully kept from the view of other members of the caretaking professions, they become visible to the pastor.

In the following encounter we have such a circumstance. A severely disturbed mother-daughter relationship was exposed when the pastor visited in the home. Also the symptoms of the disturbed emotional state of the daughter were spelled out by her response to a ceremonial event. This made it possible to bring skilled intervention into the disturbed setting. The pastor was able to serve as a mediator, resource and guide during the long and painful period when the problems were being resolved.

Thelma was an unmarried woman in her middle thirties who lived with her widowed mother. Thelma had never worked, because she had been needed at home to care for her mother, who was confined to a wheelchair because of arthritis. Thelma had attended a conservative college run by the church where she supposedly trained to be a primary schoolteacher.

Thelma's father, a retired clergyman, died shortly after Thelma completed her college education. He was a warm, quiet, loving individual, genuinely concerned about people and their needs but lacking in the personality traits that might have made him a successful minister, in terms of promotion to large and opulent parishes. So he had spent his years serving in little churches in small towns, caring for his invalid wife and supervising the strict upbringing of his only child, Thelma.

Thelma's mother had been strictly raised in a New England family of some wealth. She apparently had been shielded from any practical knowledge about sex and human sexuality. After the first few months of marriage she rejected her husband sexually, completed her one pregnancy and retreated to her wheelchair, claiming her invalidism as an escape from life and its activities. From her wheelchair she dominated the life of the family, enslaved her husband and as time went on increasingly enslaved Thelma.

The pastor of the parish in which Thelma and her mother lived visited in the home often. He sensed the artificial climate and the tension that existed between mother and daughter and the feelings of helplessness and frustration that increasingly bound Thelma, whose emotional strength at best seemed fragile. However, there seemed to be little that could be done of a corrective nature without some form of crisis to precipitate things.

One day the pastor was called by a neighbor who said, "I think there is something wrong with Thelma. Maybe you had better check it out! I have been over there, but Thelma's mother won't open the door. I haven't seen Thelma for several days. It's quite unusual, don't you think?"

The pastor went to the home immediately as if on a routine pastoral visit. After talking with Thelma's mother for a while quite casually, he asked, "How's Thelma?"

The mother twitched a bit, grimaced and fiddled with the items she had on the little desk she used with her wheelchair. As if with great difficulty she finally said, "Thelma's not acting right."

The pastor responded, "What do you mean?"

"Several days ago she went into her room, slammed the door and I haven't seen her since. I know she comes out, for I hear her moving around, but I can't get up there. At night after I'm in bed I hear her in the kitchen. But I'm keeping an eye on things and I am sure she'll be all right."

"Don't you think I should go up and talk with her?"

Thelma's mother protested: "Oh, no, that isn't necessary. It wouldn't look right for you to be up there alone with her. I'm looking out for things."

"But how are you making out? You need some help, don't you? Should I arrange for someone to come in and help you with meals and things?"

"Oh, no, I can make out all right. I'll just wait for this to pass over. Thelma is high-strung, you know, but she usually gets over things."

Feeling blocked at every point, the pastor suggested that he would stop in every day for a while, and if there was anything that she needed she should call him at once.

For several days the visits were not productive. Thelma's mother protested that everything was all right or would be soon. One day when the pastor walked up on the porch he heard loud talking and then footsteps running up the stairs. When he entered Thelma was nowhere in sight.

After about two weeks of these unproductive daily visits, one afternoon Thelma called downstairs and told the pastor she wanted to talk to him. Over the protests of the mother the pastor went upstairs and sat down with Thelma to listen to what she had to say. Thelma was bedraggled and unkempt. She looked haggard and hungry. She whispered, "We can't talk here. My mother will hear us. She is angry at me. She won't let me out of the house. Things are terrible. I'm going crazy, I think."

The pastor asked Thelma to come with him. They went downstairs, and he explained to Thelma's mother that they were going to the store and would be right back in a short while.

When they were in the car the pastor said, "Now you can talk if you want to."

Thelma said, "I can't stand it anymore. It's been terrible.

Ever since I found her out she has been threatening me, and I don't know what to do. I can't leave her and I can't stay there any longer."

"What do you mean, you found her out?"

"Oh, I came home and found her out. You know, I had never seen her out of that wheelchair all my life. I thought she couldn't get out of it. When I went to the store I forgot my grocery list, and when I rushed back in there she was hobbling around out of the chair. She was so angry. She was a completely different person. She threatened me if I ever told anyone. I don't know what to do. I don't know what to think. I just hate her, hate her, hate her. She did this to my father, and now she's doing it to me. I've got to get away, but how can I leave her?"

The pastor gave Thelma the assurance that if they worked together they would be able to find some solution to a complex problem. He tried to make it clear to Thelma that her mother was not only crippled physically but was also suffering from some crippling mental and emotional states. When they returned home with groceries the pastor talked casually with Thelma's mother and suggested that Thelma should get out of the house more. He suggested attending church services, which seemed to be the least objectionable activity he could think of from her mother's point of view.

The next Sunday Thelma was in church. It was a communion Sunday, and Thelma participated. After the service she hurried out with no comment. However, the next day's mail brought a six-page typewritten letter filled with devastating criticism of the pastor. In effect the letter said that he had done everything wrong in conducting the service. At all points the writer made comparisons with the way her father had done things when he was a pastor. The letter was rambling, illogical, angry, hostile and quite out of character, seemingly, for this timid, fragile person.

The pastor tried to analyze the letter. It carried a large measure of emotional release, and he felt reassured that she felt enough confidence in him to pour it all out as she had done. In this letter, he felt, were some clues to her emotional state. Yet he was not sure enough of his skills to try to evaluate it by himself.

The pastor called a psychiatrist at the university hospital fifty miles away and made an appointment to see the psychiatrist. He gave the psychiatrist the background of the case and showed him the letter.

The psychiatrist listened to the account of events and agreed that the mother was probably not in a position to do Thelma any physical harm but was doing her a great amount of mental and emotional damage, and that it would probably be necessary to find some way of intervening to assist Thelma. He said that the shock of finding her mother out of the wheelchair after building her whole image of her mother as a helpless invalid was great, and the full damage of that discovery would be known only after careful examination. It was his feeling that Thelma should be examined and given psychiatric help as quickly as possible to prevent further damage to her battered psyche.

The psychiatrist agreed to go with the pastor to talk with Thelma's mother, to point out to her the nature of Thelma's illness and the need for immediate intervention. Also it was necessary to arrange for care of the mother physically during the period of Thelma's examination and treatment.

When confronted by the pastor and the psychiatrist, Thelma's mother was hostile and resistant. She showed strength and skill in presenting her case. She claimed that Thelma could not live without her mother's love and care; that she had never been away from home except during the carefully sheltered years of college and that she couldn't function away from her mother's love. She further claimed that she was the only one who really understood her daughter and her needs. When none of these ploys seemed to create the desired impression she indicated that she controlled the family money and that she was not about to waste it on stupid psychiatrists who seemed to be intent upon breaking up a loving family.

The psychiatrist gently and patiently led Thelma's mother to consider the kind of sacrificial love that might be in her daughter's interest, and finally it was agreed that Thelma would go into the hospital for examination with regular reports sent to the mother through the pastor.

The first report from the psychiatrist after a week of careful

examination of Thelma's mental and emotional state was that
he had discovered a veritable chamber of psychiatric horrors.
Thelma was in intensive psychotherapy for two years, during
which time she was able to get a new idea of who she was and
what her role could be in relation to her mother. The idea that
her mother's life had been a lie was related to an awareness of
why sick people cannot tolerate the truth and so need to distort
both life and truth. The aggressive letter to the pastor concerning the communion service was Thelma's effort to come to the
defense of her dead father, because he had been so victimized by
the mother's escape into the wheelchair, which she could use as
a throne to dominate the other important people in her life.

After two years of intensive therapy Thelma was equipped to
come home and again care for her mother. Basically this was
what she wanted to do. But she did it with a new understanding
of her mother and her domineering nature. She was able to protect herself from damage, and when she felt a buildup of stress
she went back to the psychiatrist for some brief therapeutic intervention. She cared for her mother until she died in her eight-
ies and now continues to live alone in the family home, active in
church, musical and other community affairs. While she has not
lived a life of spectacular achievement, she developed new
strengths and was able to manage a distressing family situation
with some skill and perspective.

The pastor's encounter with a disturbed family in the parish
shows how some people of the parish live with life-shattering
events that are not usually marked as major tragedy but have
within them the possibility for great damage to the lives of the
people who live with the quiet but stressful human relationships
that family life can produce.

The close relationship the pastor has may make it possible for
him to see these distressing conditions and be the person in the
community who can begin to do something significant about
them. Here the aid of professional skilled resources of the larger
community may be essential to the pastoral task. Sometimes the
objectives must of necessity be limited, but part of the process of
practical diagnostics is to know the limitations within which the
healing community works toward its reasonable goals.

Chapter 17

"We've Just Run Out of Emotional Resources"

Sometimes the pastor serves as an agent to help people confront realities they would like to escape but sooner or later must confront honestly. Most of the time these decisions are rooted in deep emotions and must be met at the emotional level.

In the following encounter it quickly became evident that the deep emotions were bound up with the basic obligations of life which can produce some of the difficult conflicts of life. The pastor wanted to be free of involvement in the decision-making process, but he wanted to help the parents in working toward the decisions that they would have to live with.

The religious problems are often related to the emotional decisions of life, the right and the wrong, the blame and the guilt. While the pastor had no time to prepare in advance, he was able to move along with the parents and perhaps stay a bit ahead of their psychological movement. When people talk a lot the pastor has more time to assess what is happening and stay close to their thoughts and feelings. Some of his questions might have been put better, and the reader can imagine how he might have handled some of the comments more wisely.

Mr. and Mrs. Everts called the church office and said they would like to talk with the pastor. An agreeable time was set, and they arrived at the pastor's study on schedule.

After a few pleasantries, the pastor asked, "Now, what was it you wanted to see me about?"

The Evertses looked at each other as if to decide who was to start. Mrs. Everts said: "I suppose I might as well begin, and Harry can fill in anything that I leave out. You know about Betsy, but maybe you don't know all about her. There has always been something unusual about her. When she was just a baby we noticed that she did not respond the way the others did. At first it wasn't any big problem, because we always knew children could be a lot different even in the same family. The doctor checked her out regularly and didn't say much except that sometimes these things were outgrown. But they never were.

"It seemed that the older she got the worse she got. It was always a struggle to manage her. She didn't seem to learn how to get along. She didn't adjust. We thought when she got in school a different setting might change things, but it didn't. From the first day, it was trouble. After a few months they told us in as kind a way as they could that they couldn't keep her. The guidance teacher said that the unusual child needs an unusual school. We found such a place and took her there. But it didn't seem to make much difference where she was, it was the same story—always more trouble."

Here Mr. Everts broke in. "She was always such a lovely child to look at. Beautiful features. Lovely blond hair. You'd think she was a little angel, but there was always that cunning look in her eyes. She just had a way of outsmarting everyone, as if she had an extra sense and knew how to take advantage of people. She could get her way one way or another. And never seemed to have any feeling for anyone else. Sometimes we even felt she was possessed by a devil, the way she acted. Well, Fran, I just thought I ought to put that in. You go on."

Mrs. Everts continued: "Well, yes. She was that difficult. It was so hard, because she looked the opposite. We tried to be understanding, but it just seemed that it was impossible to understand her. We would try to punish her and it only made things worse. We tried to reward her and she took advantage of everything. In the schools it was the same way. They knew about her kind of problems, but all they would say was that she was difficult to manage. She came home for Christmas and in the summer. It sounds terrible to say it about one of your own children, but we hated to think of her coming and were so glad when we could take her back to the school.

"We'd always brief the other children. We'd say 'Betsy is coming home for Christmas and we must all work together to show her a good time. She is different from the rest of us, but she is your sister and we have to be kind to her.'

"Everyone would try hard for a day or two, but then everything would break loose. She'd find out what dolls were the girls' favorites and then would mutilate them, as if the more she could hurt others the more she liked it. So someone was always on guard, watching her. You can see why we were glad when she went back to the school. We got back to normal. This sounds terrible, but that's just the way it was.

"That went on for years. When you moved here she was a teenager. We never said much. You invited her to one of the youth picnics and that was a catastrophe. As she got older she used sex to manipulate and humiliate the boys. She seemed to have no feelings about right and wrong. It was like she lived in a different world. Well, we made sure that she didn't attend any more youth programs, but we didn't like to talk about our problem with her, and so you never got the full story.

"But now the whole thing has gotten much worse. Betsy got to the age where the school couldn't keep her anymore. It's just up to eighteen. They said we'd have to take her home or make some other provision for her. You can guess it has been costing us a fortune at that school and no real benefit—just like keeping her under observation and control all the time. So it was a state institution, and you know what they are, or another private school with all the expense, or trying to manage her at home for a while at least.

"Well, we've been trying. Five weeks and it seems like five years. We don't know what's going to happen next. She gets out and then there's all kinds of trouble. She has been picked up by the police for shoplifting. She has been complained about for seducing younger boys. She goes into rages when we try to control her—and throws things and beats us up. When you look at her she seems like a beautiful young woman, but underneath there is something so terrible we can't endure it. So we've got to come to some decision. She's ruining the family. We can't endure any more, for we are just running out of emotional resources. We hate the thought of putting her in a state institution. So here we are. We can't afford a private place, not with the other children ready for college. We are so upset we can't think straight. So Harry said why don't we talk it all over with you. So that's our story. Here we are. Harry, do you want to add anything?"

Harry said: "No, you've covered most everything. Except the other kids. They get the hard time from their friends. Questions like, 'What's with your sister?' 'Is she on dope?' And she can be dangerous. She has no license, and we don't let her have a car, but she gets them from boys, and you know how. She drives like everything else, and has had a couple of minor scrapes already. We just think it is too much all around. Is it cruel for us to put her away for her own good and everybody else's?"

The pastor assessed this story and the human pathos of parents who suffered such conflict between their natural parental feelings and their confronting of a major behavior disorder. He sensed that they were trying to do an impossible task within the home framework. But their problem was not with their knowledge but with their conflicted feelings.

So the pastor asked, "What do the doctors say about the prognosis? Can they help Betsy any?"

Mr. Everts answered: "Not really. They say her kind of problem is one of the hardest to treat, because they can't establish any point of relationship. They can control some of the aggressive behavior chemically, but of course that is only temporary. The pills wear off, and when she is home she fights them. I guess they have other means of administering the medication in an institution. But, no. They don't give us much hope. They don't seem to think she will ever be any different."

Mrs. Everts added: "They say there is research going on now and no one knows when there may be a breakthrough. But they tell us this is something so deep-seated that it is almost impossible to get to it. About all they can do with these cases is keep them from hurting themselves and other people. I'm sure it doesn't do Betsy any good to have her home. If love would help, Lord knows we've tried. But you can even run out of love when it doesn't do any good. She doesn't even seem to know what love means."

"You have said that it is difficult on the rest of the family trying to cope with Betsy and her behavior," the pastor commented. "You imply that it is doing Betsy no good but is doing the family real harm. Is that right?"

Both started to respond at once, but Mr. Everts bowed in favor of his wife. "You see, that's the worst part. The other children seem to be so sensitive. They feel so upset about this. They try to be kind to Betsy and it never works. They are baffled. Then they all want to gang up on Betsy. And that isn't any help. But you see, it isn't that simple. If we put Betsy in a private treatment center, we won't have enough money to send the others to college. So we're in a bind."

The pastor listened and then phrased the question that seemed so hard to confront. "If Betsy doesn't respond to treatment, would it make much difference in her treatment process if she were in a state institution? Would it seem valid to penalize the other children in order to provide treatment for Betsy that seems to have so little possibility of being of any use?"

Mr. Everts thought a while as tears came into his wife's eyes. Then he said: "That put it in a nutshell. Is it really fair to the healthy kids to use the resources for their education in a hopeless task with Betsy? It seems heartless to say this, but sooner or later I think we'd have to face it."

Mrs. Everts wiped her eyes. "It seems as if we have spent our whole lives trying to put off this moment," she said. "We've tried everything. We've used up our money, our energy and now our emotional strength. And for what? Things seem to keep getting worse. There has to be an end somewhere. But when I look at Betsy I can't make myself think she's hopeless."

The pastor listened in silence for a while as neither seemed to want to speak. Then he said, "We tend to identify a person with his body and its appearance. It's hard for us to realize that his behavior is rooted in things we cannot see."

"That's so true," Mrs. Everts said. "The Betsy we see isn't the same Betsy who does these terrible things all the time."

"Now, now, Fran," said Mr. Everts, "You know that doesn't make sense. Of course it is the same person. We just have to see that her behavior is the sick part of her. Her body may look healthy, but she has another form of sickness, and that is what we have to face finally. We've put that off for too long."

Again a silence, and then Mrs. Everts said: "Whichever way it goes, I know I am going to feel guilty. I've always felt that in some way I must have made her the way she is. Something I did when I was carrying her. Something I ate or some medicine that I took. Don't you think parents make their children the way they are?"

The pastor responded: "There is no doubt that parents have an important influence on their children in most instances. But there are hereditary factors, genes and things, chemical accidents, environmental influences that are well beyond a parent's control. No parent is omnipotent. Don't you think it would be unreasonable to assume blame for things you couldn't be responsible for?"

Mr. Everts broke in: "That's what I've been telling her for years. She can't keep on blaming herself. That just makes it harder to face the real problem—the whole family. If you could say something to Fran to make her forget this guilt business we might get somewhere."

"It's easy to blame yourself," the pastor said, "because we like to tack a simple cause-effect relationship to the things that happen in life. And when you have felt guilty for a long time it's hard to stop. But it doesn't make much sense to blame yourself for something you didn't do or couldn't help. That complicates all the other problems."

Mrs. Everts wiped her eyes again. "If I only thought God

could forgive me, I could forgive myself."

The pastor responded: "If God is a God of grace, why would you think you wouldn't be forgiven for something you didn't really do?"

"When you put it that way, it doesn't make much sense, does it?" Mrs. Everts said. "Would you be willing to say a prayer, just to make sure God forgives me?"

"Why, yes, I would be glad to," the pastor said. "But you know prayer isn't just words. If you pray for something it is important to accept it when it is given. I believe God is more willing to forgive than we are to accept the forgiveness, oftentimes. You would be willing to accept forgiveness if we ask for it, wouldn't you?"

"Yes, of course," she said.

"Any questions or comments before we pray?" the pastor asked.

"When I prayed for forgiveness, I didn't feel worthy of it. Maybe that's why I never accepted it. But as you said, God wouldn't blame anyone for something she didn't do. No, I don't have any questions," she said.

"All right, then. Let us be in the mood of quiet meditation and prayer. Eternal God, we are often mystified by life, and yet we know You are the source of all life. When we cannot penetrate the mystery we seek some understanding that can help us cope with what mystifies us. You know our thoughts and our problems. You know Fran's feelings of guilt. We know Your grace is unlimited and we know You are ever willing to forgive us as we forgive ourselves and others. Enter our consciousness with the forgiveness that frees us from fear and self-condemnation. Help us find the strength to do those things we believe are wise and necessary to meet the obligations of our living. Guide us in the difficult days that face us. We pray in the spirit of the Great Physician. Amen."

"Thank you so much," Mrs. Everts said. "It's like a great weight was lifted. It's not going to be easy, but I think I can see the way now. It was so good to talk with you. You have made so many things clear for us. Hasn't he, Harry?"

"Yes, thanks a lot. It's been a big help. I think we have found some strength to do what we have to do," said Mr. Everts as he guided his wife toward the door.

In this pastoral encounter it was clear that the basic problem was one of managing some deeply rooted feelings of guilt. The religious nature of the counselor was employed by the counselees in their request for prayer. The chance that this request would be made of any other professional counselor would be quite remote. But it can be valid and useful in this context and may well be one of the important resources the pastor can use in helping to get a focus beyond life-constricting emotions. And this appeared to be the effect upon the counselees.

With the pastor's privileged approach to the families of his parish he would be able to follow up with these parents to see how they were doing. He would know that not all of the problems were resolved that easily or that quickly. So he would want to have a further chance to talk about feelings and thoughts and be aware of any other emotional problems that were a part of the difficult family situation.

Chapter 18

Emotional Problems Revealed by Out-of-Wedlock Pregnancy

Sometimes the deeper emotional problems of a person are revealed by circumstances that need to be explored with them. Often the persons who come to a pastor are not members of his parish, and so he works with them initially on an emergency basis and then works out a referral to someone who is able to stay with the problem for a longer period of time.

The young woman in the following encounter had several basic problems: her home training, her loneliness and its cause, her blind spot at the point of personal responsibility and her need for careful examination of her confused attitude toward self-punishment and personal responsibility.

When she first came to the pastor her immediate needs took priority but her long-range needs determined the course of her growth toward maturity and responsibility for her thoughts and feelings.

The minister needs to be aware of the deep-rooted states of mind and emotion that underlie the behavior patterns that may first bring a person to him for pastoral care. The effects are not usually dealt with wisely, unless there is some adequate perception of the causes that are operative.

Pastoral counseling is often a strange mixture of spiritual guidance, psychological insight and social service work. This is not because the pastor would necessarily desire it that way, but rather because circumstances tend to shape the relationships that develop.

The following case combined a concern for the long-range health of a person with the immediate practical necessities. It also gave opportunity for developing ethical insight and personal responsibility. It illustrates also the kind of referral that can be made within the structure of the church so that the pastoral relationship is maintained.

"I don't know what I'm doing here really. I don't know you and you don't know me. But I have a terrible problem and I desperately need someone to talk to. At the office where I work somebody suggested I come and see you. So here I am." The young woman speaking was carefully dressed, attractive in a quiet way and quite obviously distressed.

"I am pleased that you had enough confidence in me to come with your problem," I responded. I wanted to put her at ease. I did not want to say anything that would add to her distress. I wanted her to feel that I accepted her and her problem. I could have asked who it was who suggested that she come, with the thought that we might find a common bond in a mutual friend. I might have emphasized the existence of the "terrible problem," but I did not want to build up her anxiety by giving resonance to the terrifying. I sensed her anxiety about her problem and tried to phrase my first question so that I would stay close to the problem that had brought her to me without increasing the apprehension surrounding it by giving it a "terrible" connotation. in my words. So I said, "What was it you felt the need to talk about?"

Ordinarily I would not have moved as directly to the primary concern, but would have let her determine the pace at which she would move in communicating. But her anxiety was so apparent that any delay in getting to it could easily have been interpreted as diversion, or as discomfort on my part, so I chose to move directly toward her concern.

"I'm quite sure I'm pregnant. I'm a long way from home and I don't want to get my parents upset. I don't have any close friends. I've only been in the city for a few months. I like my job and I'm doing well at it. Now this happens. I don't know what to do. Everything could fall to pieces. I've made a mess of things."

Her elaboration on her problem confirmed her anxiety, and the threat to the things she held valuable. It became quite clear that her initial purpose in coming to me was a wish that some miracle could be performed and she would be free of her problem, would admit having learned an important lesson, and then could go on with her life largely untouched by what had happened. She wanted to preserve the things she felt were valuable but did not appear to see clearly the relationship between things as they were and the value structure within which she desired to live. It seemed important now to move away from the miracle worker role she would place upon me without destroying her confidence, and at the same time help her toward a realistic acceptance of the nature of her problem and her responsibility in relation to it.

Her statement about pregnancy was not certain. Her statement about her parents was ambiguous. Her lack of close friends might be a significant clue to her problem. Her statement about making a "mess of things" might be a starting point toward assuming responsibility for her behavior, but I was not sure as yet. I did not want to pose any further threat to her at this point, so I made a response that kept the door open for further elaboration without indicating any direction to the conversation. I said, "I understand what you meant when you said you have a problem, and I think I can understand the deep concern you have about it. You must have been thinking about every aspect of your problem almost steadily."

"That's right," she responded instantly. "I can't seem to think about anything else. And the more I think about it the more confused I get, because I don't know what to do and I don't know anybody and there is no one to talk it over with. I just seem to go around in circles until my mind is whirling and I never come up with anything worthwhile. I get desperate, and sometimes I feel anything is better than trying to face this thing alone."

Here she confirmed the degree of her anxiety by describing her state of mind and emotion as a whirling confusion. She was evidently not able to do constructive thinking about her problem. The veiled threat of suicide confirmed both her confusion and her desperation. However, the most obvious thing about her statement was that three times she emphasized her aloneness. One of the most obvious facts about a pregnancy is that it is not a unilateral venture. However, no reference had been made to a man. It seemed safe to assume that she felt doubly threatened in her condition because she had been rejected, or felt she would be, by the man involved. As each of her statements so far had emphasized this aloneness, it was reasonable to assume that my next move might be designed to help her verbalize her lonely feelings. So I said, "You speak of facing this alone. Just how do you mean?" I knew immediately that I had made a wrong lead, for a frightened look came into her eyes. She gave an involuntary jerk that shook her whole body. She looked at me, then away, and then back at me again. Then there was a long pause as if she were manufacturing an answer rather than just pouring out her feelings.

Then she said, "I know what you are thinking. And you are right. And that is the hardest part of it. I really knew better, but it was all so strange and big and lonely that I was caught off guard. He seemed so kind and genuine and warm and loving, and he was such good fun . . ." Here there was a long pause, and obviously a change in the emotions being felt. With a burst of anger she said, "If I live to be a hundred I'll never forget what he said. He just laughed at me and said, 'That's your problem kiddo. Didn't you ever hear about pills? How was I to know you were just from the sticks? I thought you knew your way around.' Oh, how I hate him. To laugh, oh, how his laugh cut through me. I still hear it. At night I wake up hearing him laugh. I am afraid to go to sleep for fear I will hear it."

Then for a long time she poured out her hatred and her hurt. She at times seemed to take satisfaction in her rejection, as if she were accepting a deserved punishment. At other times she stopped to wipe her eyes when describing her hurt. But most of this lengthy venting of feeling centered on her hatred of the man who laughed at her. From this outpouring came several things that were carefully noted. While I was quite sure that I could have made a better lead into this material, the end result seemed to be on the plus side, for she got directly into the more difficult material of thought and feeling. She seemed relieved to be able to express such strong feelings with safety. However, she said three things that I marked for future consideration. One was the statement, "My mother warned me never to trust a man." Another was, "Every time I look at my child I will see that brute laughing at me." The third was, "Why do things like this have to happen to me, when other girls are getting away with things all the time?" The first probably was a key to an emotional background that would need to be explored before her attitudes toward men could achieve any real maturity. The second statement would have considerable bearing on her emotions as she approached a decision on adoption. The third statement indicated something of her ethical orientation at the level where she actually lived. All implied unfinished business in the developing of a mature and competent self.

After this major outpouring of thought and feeling, she acted emotionally spent. I did not want to change the mood, but there seemed no inclination to proceed further. I wanted to close the interview with a constructive emphasis, and one that would naturally lead into another interview, for I was quite sure that we were both aware of unfinished business. She sat quietly for some time. I sensed that it was changing from a relaxed and comfortable silence to rather an embarrased silence, so I went back to a lead that I had been saving for this time. I said, "When you were talking earlier you said that you were quite sure that you were pregnant. Don't you think it's important to find out?"

She responded that she wanted to but did not know any physicians. We worked out some arrangements for an interview with a physician. His judgment was that consideration for her health made it advisable for the pregnancy to run its course. During several interviews we explored the relationships of her life, her attitudes toward her parents, her feelings about herself and the basis of her relationship to other people.

At the practical level we arranged for her to take a position as a filing clerk in a medical records office of a church-related hospital. She made plans for the adoption of her baby through the adoption agency related to the hospital.

At the personal level, she gained a great deal of insight into the emotional factors of her own background. She saw in the basically unsatisfactory sex relation between her parents a factor that she had not properly evaluated and so had tended to overcompensate in her own behavior. She was able to think through her standards of judgment as to what makes a desirable man. She was able to accept her own feelings of self-judgment not with remorse but as a basis for evaluating experience.

After she was employed in the hospital the counseling relationship was transferred to the hospital chaplain, who was given the complete background of her experience. He saw her through the final months of her pregnancy and the details of the adoption. In fact, she became so interested in hospital work that she is still at it three years later. She plans to marry one of the administrative staff at the hospital in the near future.

I visited her at the hospital occasionally when making other calls there. Two things were brought up that may be worth mentioning in conclusion. We had never worked through the matter of what she should tell her parents, if anything. She mentioned quite casually one day, "You remember how we talked about what we should do about telling my parents. Well, I never had to say anything about it, and it is probably better that way, for I am quite sure they would never have understood."

The other comment was rather revealing, not so much of her as of the church. She said: "One night before I came to see you the first time, I was feeling desperate. I was walking the street thinking of the river. I stopped in front of a church. I saw some lights in an upstairs apartment and thought maybe there was somebody there who would talk with me. I crossed the street and rang the bell. Someone opened an upstairs window and shouted down, 'What do you want?' I said I had a problem and wanted to talk to someone. The voice shouted back, 'The ministers have all gone home and that's where you should be. All good little girls should be in bed by now. If you still want to talk tomorrow come back at a sensible hour.' Well, I never went back. Considering how I felt about churches and ministers that night, I can't quite understand why I ever went to see you. But I'm glad I did."

The encounter of the pastor with people in need is not apt to fall into the orderly bounds of an appointment book. The calls upon the shepherd come when the sheep are hurt and in need. The pastor is really never "off duty."

Chapter 19

"I Can't Seem to Find God Anymore"

When people want to talk with the pastor about a religious problem he should be alert to what lies behind their concern. The emotional problem often surfaces first in what they think of as a spiritual matter.

In the following encounter the pastor was used primarily as a sounding board. As the counselee talked he heard himself. He had talked with himself often before but had not heard all that he was saying. Now, with someone to listen, he found another dimension for his words. And this precipitated the action he had been wanting to take but had not found the resources for taking.

The circumstances seemed to be casual. But part of the genius of parish counseling is the accessibility that comes with this casualness. When it is difficult to approach someone with a problem, it seems to make it easier when you are working together and have some other points of common interest.

George was a member of a cleanup squad, a group of men who lived in apartments but liked to spend Saturday mornings doing odd jobs out of doors around the church. They assisted the property committee and seemed to have fun and exercise at the same time. George was cleaning out debris that had collected in the boxwood hedge, and the pastor had the same task in the azalea garden. George came over to the pastor and said, "Any chance I could chat with you a while during the coffee break?"

"Yes, I think so," responded the pastor. "Let's sit over there on the stone fence where we might be less apt to be interrupted."

About an hour later they were sitting together engaging in some small talk about people who throw beer cans in hedges and show no respect for public property. When that line of conversation ran thin, George said, "You know, I've been wanting to talk with you for a while. It's nothing serious, but it bothers me."

"Well, let's explore it," the pastor said.

"It's about prayer. When I pray it seems as if God isn't there anymore. God doesn't seem to be real anymore. I can't seem to find God when I want to."

"I see. Something seems to have happened to your relationship to God. Some change has taken place. What was the relationship like before this change?"

"Oh, always before it was, you know, simple and direct. It was like talking to somebody who was there. Now it's like talking to somebody who isn't there," George commented.

"Yes, I think I see what you mean. Prayer is a form of communication. Two are involved. If one end of the communication breaks down it doesn't seem to work. But the problem is often to find out which end of the communication is in trouble," the pastor remarked.

George looked puzzled. "I don't know what you're getting at. I never had any trouble before. It always seemed to work for me. Now it doesn't. Maybe you're trying to say there's something the matter with me. Is that it?"

"What I'm trying to do is find out where the trouble is. Has there been some change in you that might have caused a fracturing in the relationship between you and God? What makes the difference?"

"Oh, that's it." George thought a while. "Now I think I see what you're getting at. You mean God probably stays the same, but I've had a change. Well, that certainly brings it right close to where we are."

The pastor made no comment but continued to listen with intentness. George thought quite awhile. Then he continued: "I'm trying to think when this happened. I guess it came on gradually. I didn't notice it until I really needed to pray hard. And I felt lost—the contact was broken. When Emily had that sick spell, you remember, well, it looked pretty bad at first and I felt so helpless and I tried to pray and, I don't know, it just seemed like I was talking to myself. I didn't get any of the good feelings I used to get."

"Yes, I remember that time. I prayed with you at the hospital then. But it didn't seem to have the meaning you wanted. Well, we're narrowing it down a bit. That was when you first became aware of a change."

"That's when I had the feeling that prayer wasn't doing any good. If the doctors couldn't do it, we were in trouble. There wasn't anything else to bank on," George answered.

"Before this time of Emily's illness, can you think of anything that might have affected your spiritual life—the attitudes you had, the things you said and did that could give us some clues to the change?"

George sat quite a while thinking. Finally he said, "Yes, there are some things that made me uneasy." He looked at this pastor questioningly as if he didn't know whether or not he should elaborate. The pastor said nothing, and after a while George continued.

"This new position I took a couple of years ago isn't all I thought it would be. I've had to make some adjustments. Some of them were tough on me." A further pause.

"How so?" the pastor finally asked.

More pause. George acted uncomfortable. He rubbed his hands and squirmed. Then he said, "It's kind of a long story. I doubt if you want to hear it."

"If you want to tell me about it, of course I'd be interested. But if you do not want to talk about it, it's your privilege. But either way, it might be significant for what we've been talking about."

"I don't follow that."

"It's just that the things that are hard to talk about may have emotional meaning. We can explore it, but we can't ignore it. Either way it has meaning that you may want to take into account. But you're the one to decide that, how and when and with whom," the pastor tried to reassure George.

"Okay, I might as well spill it. Anytime you can't take anymore, just say so and I'll clip it." George readjusted his seat on the stone fence as if looking for a softer spot. Then he continued: "You know I took a new job a couple of years ago. It was with a couple of fellows I knew in school. It looked good. More money and a fancy title. And I needed it. Payments on the house and with Joe and Jan both in college at the same time. Director of expansion services. What does that sound like to you?"

George went on to answer his rhetorical question.

"I knew it was a growing industry, and I felt good to be invited to be a part of the action. My experience in research and development seemed to fit the new job, but it wasn't quite like that. It wasn't long before I began to get the picture. We'd move in on people who had some of the patents we wanted, show goodwill, invest in their development and, when they were overextended, put the pressure on. Most of the time we'd be able to work out a merger, but the terms were brutal. It was supposed to look like we were saving them, but really we were destroying them. Our methods were the picture of corporate efficiency. We had the best legal staff imaginable. Everything was legal. But it was brutal . . ."

George shuddered a bit, then went on: "It's like this. We'd move in on a company. They'd have a lot of money tied up in pension funds. We'd say, 'Get rid of everybody over sixty before they make claims on the pension funds.' Lots of these people couldn't get any kind of a job again. They counted on the pension. Through a merger we could change the corporate structure so that we could take over the assets of these companies and slide out from under many of their liabilities. All legal, of course.

"I was the one who had to engineer this whole process. I had to meet lots of these people. I heard their stories. I had to say over and over again that there was nothing we could do for individuals. We just bought the company. So sorry. But you know, it got to me. I never was in a deal like that. We did three of these things the first year. All clever and legal. And if you watch the stock market, you know it paid off. We moved up when lots of other things were going the other way.

"I felt so damned mean. In board meetings I would make comments about methods and got laughed at. 'Going soft— George, the chicken-hearted.' That got to me also. I guess I was feeling guilty about all these things. When Jan came home from college and said one of her sorority sisters was dropping out of college because her father had lost his job in a merger, it hit me. Oh, it wasn't one of our mergers, thank goodness, but I got the message.

"When Emily was taken ill with that mysterious disease, I had the feeling that God was punishing me through the suffering of an innocent person. I really wanted to curse God instead of pray. I was so caught up in all of this. I couldn't get out. I couldn't get another position like it and we needed all I was making. I was caught. I got the best doctors and paid them well to do what they did. And you know so well, Emily came through all right. But I was vulnerable. I really wasn't happy. I felt boxed in. I didn't sleep well. I began drinking too much. The whole thing was disrupting my life, my values, my family, my health . . ."

"Yes, you had really gone through quite a change," the pastor commented.

"No, you're wrong. If I had changed enough everything would have been all right. My damned conscience wouldn't lie down and be quiet. I watched the other members of the board. Nothing seemed to bother them. They seemed to be happy. They didn't feel any guilt. I kept asking myself, why was I so vulnerable? I tried to suppress my feelings. I thought I would get used to things in time. But I kept getting more and more upset and desperate. I tried to pray and it didn't work. So I tried a new form of meditation. At first I thought it was working, but then my conscience came blasting through again. So here I am. Quite a study, isn't it? Quite a confession, I mean."

"Yes, I think we can see why it has become difficult to pray. You've made it quite clear that it is even difficult for you to live with yourself. Now that you have spilled things, we may be able to explore your problems and your inner being to see if there are some solutions," the pastor said.

"Oh, I think I know what the solution is. That comes through loud and clear. I never heard this thing out loud before. I never talked to Emily or the kids about it. It would have shocked her beyond belief. I kept it in, until just now when I spilled it on you. I know what has been happening. I've been destroying the self I have respected. I always tried to do the decent thing. I wanted to be honest and open and humane. I never wanted to be devious, cruel and calloused. It isn't worth it. I have to live with myself, don't I? If I can't live with myself I can destroy myself. That's why I'm so vulnerable, isn't it?"

George continued: "I'm going home and talk to Emily and the kids. They're home this weekend. I'll tell it to them just like I did to you, and then I'll tell them I am going to resign and look for something else. I'm sure they would support me. They always liked me the way I was, and I know they wouldn't want me to change so much that they wouldn't even know me."

George shifted himself some more, as if the stone fence were beginning to get to him also. He looked at the pastor and addressed him with almost solemnity. "I don't know how to thank you for what you've done. You've certainly clarified a lot of things for me. You've made it clear what I should do. I felt all along that was it, but I needed someone to verify it for me. Thanks a lot. You'll see us all tomorrow."

This encounter illustrates two things that the pastor must be aware of. One is that many persons in trying to solve the problems of their lives come to a time when they want to hear themselves talking about the problem. This tends to give confirmation in their minds about the validity of what they have been thinking but have not put into words. The pastor needs to say little or nothing, but he does have to be a concerned listener.

The second thing is that the pastor is always saying something by being who he is. The fact that he represents certain ethical values and moral concepts has its impact without verbalization. If he can realize this it may save him from saying some unnecessary or even unwise things to a counselee. His representative capacity may be at work for him more than he realizes. George apparently responded both ways—to the pastor's presence and to the pastor's concerned listening.

Chapter 20

Social and Psychological Implications of Illness

Illness may have many dimensions. It is not only a physical distress. It may affect all of the aspects of living. The person with illness needs a chance not only to talk about feelings but also to relate to other people in socially meaningful ways.

Sometimes the diseases that are not serious physically can be serious socially and emotionally. The pastor may be instrumental in reversing the movement toward self-pity and depression by moving toward people and bridging the gaps that exist in human relations.

Also he may be able to use his faith in the power of spiritual resources to give emotional support to those who feel emotionally defeated. The following pastoral encounter is concerned with the emotional and social implications of illness. Spiritual intervention may well have been a factor in the regression of the ailment.

When the pastor arrived at his office there was a message to call the home of Mrs. Botsford. When the pastor returned the call Mrs. Botsford asked if it would be possible for the pastor to call on her at her home. A time was agreed upon and the pastor arrived at the appointed time.

When Mrs. Botsford opened the door it was obvious that she had heavy coatings of medication on her face, arms and legs. After they were seated she began: "I am sorry that I had to call you to come here, but as you can see I'm in no condition to go out. About the only time I leave the house now is when I go to the dermatologist each week. As you can guess I have psoriasis, and that's what I want to talk to you about."

The pastor replied: "Yes, I see. I am sure you find it a most disagreeable ailment. What was it you wanted to talk about?"

Mrs. Botsford gave a little halfhearted laugh. "Maybe it was I wanted to talk with one human being that I thought could understand how desperate my condition is. I look ugly, don't I?" Without waiting for an answer Mrs. Botsford went on: "Well, I feel ugly. I know I give people the creeps when they look at me. I can see it in their eyes and in their little winces."

The pastor commented, "Yes, that must be distressing."

"This thing is affecting everything in my life. For a while I tried to go out. I would wear long sleeves and slacks and doctor up my face, but it didn't do much good. It showed through. The final blow was when I was checking out some fruit in the supermarket and the attendant yelled at me, 'Don't touch the fruit, lady!' It was like I was dirty, contaminated—a carrier of some loathsome disease like leprosy. I just left my half-filled cart and walked out of the place, and I haven't been in the store since."

"Sometimes without realizing it people can be so cruel and thoughtless," the pastor responded.

Mrs. Botsford continued: "Even things at home are different. The house used to be full of children most of the time and our game room was the local gathering center on rainy days. No more. I don't know what the children say. I don't know what the other mothers say. But things are different. They aren't here anymore, that's for sure. My neighbors call over the fence if they see me in the yard, but they don't come over for coffee like they used to. And they are all smart people. They should know it isn't catching. The worst thing they could do to me is systematically exclude me when I need to be included at least somewhere."

Mrs. Botsford paused a while as if deciding on what she should say next and then continued. "My husband is a very kind and loving person. I know he wouldn't deliberately say or do anything to hurt me. But he does, all the time. Our love life has gone to pot. He acts like he was afraid to touch me. He makes out like he's trying to be considerate but he acts like he can see in the dark. That hurts most of all. Everybody seems to forget that I am still the same person with the same feelings and needs. It's like the whole damned world was ganged up against me. I don't know how much longer I can stand it. I think I'm starting to break up myself."

"There is a steady buildup of stress, I am sure," the pastor commented. "How do you mean, you feel you are breaking up?"

"Oh, I don't know. I spend an awful lot of time just sitting. I can't wash dishes. I get simple meals. I just sit and feel sorry for myself. I keep thinking of how I used to be and how I am now. And I know I'm changing. I am curt. I say sharp things. All my nerves seem to be close to the surface. I'm so touchy and I never was that way. Everybody used to say I was too easygoing. But no more. I'm getting to be a real bitch and I know it. But I don't seem to care that much. Everybody's turned against me." Here Mrs. Botsford began to weep quietly and for several minutes said nothing.

During this period of weeping the pastor walked over to the straight chair on which Mrs. Botsford was sitting in rather stiff manner, put his right hand on her shoulder and his left hand on her bare forearm where the psoriasis was quite pronounced, and stood quietly there until her sobbing had subsided. Then he returned to his chair, and Mrs. Botsford asked, "Why did you do that?"

"I don't have a very good answer, I guess. I just felt an impulse to do it. I feel so concerned about you and your inner misery."

"Well, thank God there's someone who isn't afraid of me. I have felt such a need for a human touch. Even relatives who are sympathetic stay clear." Then she was quiet and thought a while before she said, "don't tell me you felt like Jesus touching the lepers."

"No," the pastor responded, "I was thinking more about you than I was about Jesus at that moment. But I am sure that Jesus had great faith in the power of spirit to communicate healing and redeeming love. And I would never feel it was out of my field of pastoral concern to communicate that form of healing acceptance of you and your condition."

Mrs. Botsford looked quizzical for a while and said, "You really believe that, don't you? Since I have been sitting around with nothing much to do I read your book on understanding prayer. You really think prayer can change things and people, don't you?"

"Yes, I feel prayer can help to release resources in the life of an individual. I've seen so many times when it has happened. I think it can bring into life spiritual resources with great power to change things."

"I sure wish you would use some of that magic on me. I could stand to have some things change."

"Actually, I don't think there is anything magical about it. I don't even think that prayer produces miracles. To my way of thinking the person is the miracle. Prayer works to release the power in the individual that moves him toward wholeness. I never ask for anything, because I believe it is already there. I seek ways of discovering the miraculous power for reorganization of life and regeneration of the fractured conditions of life."

"Will you pray for me?" Mrs. Botsford asked.

"Of course, I will pray with you and for you. But prayer is such an important activity that I think we should take some time to prepare for it. Is that all right?"

"Surely. Tell me how. I read the book, but I've really never tried to do anything about it. I gather it is a strenuous discipline."

"Some people have a natural endowment for this thing, and others do have to work pretty hard at it. But first we need to relax. Let your muscles fall limp. Do it deliberately—hands and feet, arms and legs, shoulders and neck—work at it awhile until you feel completely free from any muscular tension, even your jaw muscles. Now when you feel physically relaxed take the next step and relax your mind and emotions—shake loose your worries and fears, the self-pity and the anger, the anxiety and despair. That's a big order, and it's not easy—you probably can't do it all at once. But work at it for a while. Put some other thoughts and feelings to work. Patience with other people's ignorance, understanding of their fears, acceptance of their shortcomings. Now how do you feel?" This process of relaxation had taken ten or fifteen minutes, and the pastor guided it with his instructions.

Mrs. Botsford said: "I feel calm and peaceful. I think I'm more relaxed now than I've been in a long time. It's funny how tension creeps up on you."

"Yes, and you can do this anytime you want to, once you know how and sense the value of it."

The pastor went on: "Now that you are relaxed, I want to explain to you the next step. I'll stand behind your chair, put my hands lightly on your head and hold them there in silence for a while. Then I may say a few words that I trust will have prayerful meaning. Any questions?"

"No. Go ahead. I'm ready."

After five or six minutes with the laying on of hands, the pastor said: "Healing spirit at work in and through us. We seek the release of healing energy in Mrs. Botsford's being to organize and direct the life of each cell so that they will function in accordance to Thy creative plan. Let there be a release from anxiety and stress. Let there be a new purpose and direction for the energy of life. Let the energy move toward healing rather than abnormal cell growth. And let us celebrate the wonder of life with peace and joy. In the name of the Great Physician, we pray, so be it."

Mrs. Botsford turned around smiling and said: "That was wonderful. The touching part made the prayer seem more real and personal. I just sort of tingled all over. Maybe that was the new life at work that you mentioned."

"Could be," the pastor said. "And you can direct your own thoughts prayerfully whenever you want to. I am sure it can change many things for the better.

"Do you know Gloria Phillips?" the pastor continued. "She
lives over on Kendall Place. You two ought to get together. She
had psoriasis about three years ago. Had a frightful time with it.
Understands all about it. Is all cleared up now, but I know she is
working with one of her neighbors who is in an active stage. Why
don't you call her? She'd be glad to hear from you. Tell her I
suggested it. Her phone is listed under her husband's name, Ar-
thur. They're both great people. It would be good for your social
life."

Mrs. Botsford said that she felt so much better; she would call
Gloria and would surely call the pastor again if she had further
matters to talk over with him.

Within two weeks the disorder had shown marked improve-
ment, with the crustation largely replaced by red blotches that
her dermatologist said would also rapidly disappear.

The three women, who met together for a social time one
morning a week, continued and expanded their activity. They
asked the pastor to let them know whenever he came across
anyone with that troublesome disorder. They would make sure
that the sufferer could find someone to talk with who would be
understanding and helpful.

In this encounter with Mrs. Botsford it was possible to bring
together several of the resources available to the pastor. He
could call in the home, he could use psychological insight in
counseling, he could use the spiritual intervention of prayer for
wholeness of being, and he could use the group resources for
giving insight and strength. This illustrates not only the unique-
ness of the pastoral relationship but also the variety of resources
that can be used individually or collectively.

Chapter 21

A Case of
False Spirituality

Many abnormal emotional states are misinterpreted by those afflicted as having special religious meaning. Sometimes the conditions are of serious proportions and indicate psychotic states. At other times they may be quite distressing to the persons involved without presenting severe treatment problems. Part of the distress may come from the confusion of the abnormal emotional states with what seem to be religiously important motivations. Because of the religious aspect of these problems they often come to the attention of pastors, and because of the complex nature of the problems they are among the more difficult to cope with.

In the problem under consideration here two goals seemed to emerge from the interview. The first was to assess the emotional dynamics at work and gain some clues as to the severity of these conditions. The second was to create a mood on the part of the

counselee that would make referral both possible and constructive.

Mrs. Robinson made an appointment through the church office. When she presented herself at the pastor's study she gave
the appearance of one who was quite sure of herself. She was
well dressed, and carefully groomed and had an air of command
about her.

"It was good of you to see me," she stated. "I heard you speak
on the spiritual life at Hampton House (a retreat center), and I
felt I had something that I could share with you and you would
appreciate its importance. There aren't many people you can
talk to about spiritual things, you know."

She went on in an ingratiating way with a vitality of speech
and action that belied her years, for I judged she was sixty or
older. I remembered seeing her but had never had any conversation with her before and knew nothing about her apart from
what she revealed in appearance, acts, attitudes and words.

She continued: "I have always been interested in spiritual
things. My family has not had much sympathy with my turn of
mind. They are all practical, and successfully so, if I must say so.
Years ago a medium told me that I had great psychic potential,
and I have been very sensitive to other people. While I would not
say I am a mind reader, I have an uncanny way of knowing what
they are thinking about. Sometimes this gets me in trouble.
[Here she laughed rather extravagantly.] Another medium told
me that I had a blue aura, which means that I have the gift of
healing. And I think that is probably true, for I often seem to be
able to make people feel better by talking with them. And, you
know, lots of people come to me just to talk. At parties they
seem to want to get off in a corner with me to talk, and always
about some problems. That's because they sense my understanding of their inner beings, don't you think? I've always had
the feeling that I should put this spiritual resource of mine to
work for the glory of God. I have offered to help some ministers
in my own hometown, but they weren't very spiritual-minded
and didn't have any place for my special gifts in their programs.
I tell you this so that you'll know that I'm not just the ordinary
kind of person—always running to ministers with problems. I

have an unusual spiritual situation, and I'm quite sure you would be interested in it."

Here she turned the full power of her personality into a smile and beamed at me as if she were a queen about to grant a boon to a subject. I had been trying to understand what she was saying about herself as she went along. I got the cue from the two colleagues who had resisted her offers of spiritual assistance. I sensed the resistance of her family. I noticed the great pains she took to tell me that she was no ordinary person, and that her problem was unique because it was so spiritual. Also I sensed her interest in the occult from her reference to psychic sensitivities. But nothing that I took as indicative clues had been presented yet, so my comment was designed to show my interest and help her elaborate on what she probably had come to see me about in the first place. So I said, "You speak of an unusual spiritual situation. Yes, I am interested."

"My highly developed spiritual sensitivity is not something that just happened. I spend many hours in meditation and I read spiritual classics. I have a whole library of the finest spiritual material from the time of the Rhineland mystics down to Rufus Jones and Thomas Kelly. I would be a Quaker myself if my family were not so stubborn about such things. We have to go to a status church, you know. The Quakers have little enough status, God bless them. You must come over sometime and browse through my spiritual library. I know you'd enjoy it.

"Well, as I was starting to say, I don't just happen to be spiritual. I have worked at it for years, and the older I get the more important it is to me. I feel I have a great spiritual potential that must be used. Don't you think that is what the Master meant when He told us to let our light shine? Well, I do. And to be able to do it all the better, I went into the city to take a course in spiritual development. It was fabulous. We learned how to concentrate on the spiritual. This is the way guidance comes, you know, by concentration, and putting first the Kingdom of God and His righteousness. If you focus on God completely, you make it possible to hear the still, small voice speaking clearly. I was one of the best in our class, and by the end of the course I could control my mind so that I could hear God speaking to me above the confusion all around me. This is not so much a gift as it is a discipline, but I had the gift to begin with, so the discipline made me doubly sensitive."

Here she paused to see how I was taking it. I was a willing listener, but I was increasingly concerned about what I was hearing. So I merely said, "Yes, go on."

"But you know as well as I do that the good things in life are never unmixed blessings. Because I was doubly sensitive I had a double burden and a double responsibility. I was guided to say and do things that other people didn't like. I was sure I was doing God's will and following His guidance, but it didn't seem to make any difference to others. You can't stop doing the right just because it is difficult, can you? You can't turn your back on the guidance of God. But I think I became timid, and that is where the trouble began." Her mood of arrogance and self-assurance now seemed to be displaced by apprehension.

"So you became timid, and the trouble began. How do you mean?"

"Well, it's a long story but it all has to do with my daughter-in-law, who is an unspiritual person if you ever saw one." Here she went into a lengthy description of her son's wife and her interests and behavior. She told how she was guided to speak directly, openly and honestly to her about the way she conducted her family's affairs, and to plead with her for the salvation of her soul. According to her description, the intervention was not kindly received and led to a rather severe breach of family relationships. She had become the storm center. At first she had held her ground as one doing God's will, nothing more and nothing less. But finally it seemed that sanctions were employed which kept the grandchildren from making their regular visits, and a strained feeling grew up. In response to this use of sanctions, Mrs. Robinson felt obliged to make amends. She apologized, and it was at this point that the real trouble began.

"It all has to do with my guiding voice," she went on. "It used to speak to me when I concentrated and listened, but now it is driving me out of my mind. I can't get away from it. It even wakes me up in the middle of the night. It nags me constantly. It chides me gently sometimes, and then again it tears me to pieces. I have tried everything I know. I am against medicine, but I took sleeping pills to get some rest, but it didn't make any difference. The voice kept right on, and when I would not pay attention, it began talking to another voice and this conversation went on hour after hour right inside of me. I couldn't read, or work, or sleep or pray. It just takes over and it has me in such a state I cannot endure it. It is talking to me right now, saying I shouldn't be here, because you can't do me any good. How am I ever going to get away from this voice?"

The self-assurance and the delight in spiritual things now had disappeared, and a thoroughly distraught individual sat before me. The transformation of the half-hour had been dramatic, for the vivacious and young-acting woman now seemed tired and beaten.

Without waiting for me to say anything she went on: "The worst part of it all now is that this voice has turned into a devil. It says the most scandalous things about my daughter-in-law and other members of the family. Sometimes it just laughs at me so that I want to strangle it. But what can I do? I've got to get rid of this thing in me or I can't endure it much longer."

Because she assumed a knowledge of spiritual disciplines it would be difficult to try to talk with her about the uses of the normal spiritual devices for modifying the content of the lower levels of consciousness. I was well convinced now that she had employed processes similar to self-hypnosis to release some of the content of her subconscious mind, and it was having an overpowering effect upon her total being. I felt that it had taken an overpowering despair to bring this rather haughty woman with strong spiritual pretensions to the place where she would admit that things were out of control within her. She had said enough to make it quite clear that she had employed this form of pseudo-spirituality as an escape from a family situation where she felt uncomfortable, and then had used the same pseudo-spirituality as a device for justifying her aggression. From what she said, the roots of this thing ran back many years, which meant that it would need skilled handling. It seemed to me that the content of her self-revelation made it clear that she would probably accept help more readily from a specialist related to

the Jungian School, which has given special study to the manifestations of spiritual phenomena. But she had said she was
against medicine. It might mean she was against the psychiatric
branch of medicine. I felt it was a case for referral, but I had to
try to move toward referral so that she would cooperate and so
that the therapist would have a positive response from the patient to begin with.

"I can see how distressing this must be to you. I am quite sure
that there is something that can be done, but it will call for your
full cooperation," I said.

"In the state I'm in, I'm ready to try anything."

"I'd like to arrange for you to talk with Dr. Jones. I know him
well, and he has spoken at Hampton House. He has made a special study of the lower levels of consciousness, and their relation
to the spiritual life." Then I asked if she would like me to call
and try to arrange an appointment.

"Is he a psychiatrist?" she asked. "If he is, I don't want anything to do with him. My husband got me to one once and I said
then, 'Never again.' "

"Yes, Dr. Jones is a psychiatrist, and a highly competent one.
When I work with people where I feel I need help, I call on him
quite often. I am not competent to deal with the problems and I
want to do the best I know how for my people. That is why I call
on him. I can understand why you do not want to repeat an unpleasant experience, but it would not make good sense, would it,
to judge all psychiatrists by one unpleasant experience in the
past?"

"You say he spoke at Hampton House?" She pondered.
"That must mean he is not the ordinary psychiatrist. I didn't
hear him. I usually get to their lectures, but I must have missed
him. You think he is good? You think he can help me?"

"Yes, that is my only reason for suggesting it. He may send
you back to me with some suggestions as to how to proceed. But
I would feel better if I knew his judgment. Then perhaps we
could work together toward a relief of this distressing state of
being that has developed in you. Do you want me to call him?
Will you talk with him when I get him?"

"All right," she said. "Go ahead. I'll take your advice, but I would like it better if you worked together. I've had the feeling the last few days that there must be something radically wrong. I guess I'd better face it. Yes, I'll talk to him."

After getting through to Dr. Jones, I said (completely in the hearing of Mrs. Robinson): "Dr. Jones, do you have a minute? With me here in my study is a Mrs. Robinson who has been to Hampton House often. She is quite disturbed about a voice that keeps talking inside of her almost constantly. I've suggested that she talk with you about it. Will you speak with her now?"

She took the phone and after a few words said, "All right. At seven this evening. Thank you, doctor."

My purpose in talking with the psychiatrist in her presence was to give her a chance to know what I had said and to make it possible for her to feel comfortable in approaching him. It seemed to me that it was particularly important for her to make a good impression, as if she were buttressed by her appearance and the feeling that people would think her someone special. I did not want to say or do anything to damage this feeling of hers. I mentioned the doctor's interest in the retreat center to give a common bond and also to make her feel that he was not only a competent physician but also a person with a special interest in the spiritual life.

It is interesting to note how often a so-called spiritual state is used to cloak emotional problems. With an older person this is probably so well defined a defense that it is unwise to challenge it directly. In this whole interview I said nothing to confirm or deny the validity of her spiritual condition. To have questioned its validity would probably have thrown her into a defensive mood. To have confirmed it would probably have made it difficult to proceed with a referral, for she would have been less inclined to expose the distressing nature of her problem.

It is interesting also to note that she responded well to psychotherapy. While I had several conversations with the psychiatrist, I did not have any further communication with Mrs. Robinson until I received a Christmas card several months later with the following brief note on it: "Dr. Jones is a simply charming gentleman. We have gotten along famously. Hope to see you sometime at Hampton House."

Dr. Jones felt that the use of intensive meditation as an escape from some of the problems of life could with certain types of personality produce complications. Apparently Mrs. Robinson had a schizoid tendency in her nature which had never developed to the place where it caused her serious difficulty. However, her intensive meditation lowered the threshhold between her conscious mind and other dimensions of consciousness and allowed the overflow of repressed hostilities and inner conflicts in the form of the voices she mentioned. The feeling that she was being spiritual gave warrant for her aggressiveness but did not permit the normal restraints that are a part of wise human relations. When things began to fall apart the excuse of spirituality no longer served her, and the need for specialized help became apparent.

Chapter 22

The Threat
of Adolescence

One of the difficult times of life for all concerned is adolescence. The teenager tends to be uncertain and conflicted, so that his behavior is difficult to interpret. Sometimes it is aggressive and defiant. At other times it is diffident and poorly directed. What appears to be so baffling is often experimental, and some of the earlier ways of doing things in childhood are restated in a larger social circle. If rebellion seemed to bring desirable results for the three-year-old in his family relationships, he may very well try rebellion in the larger circle of life at thirteen. Through his experimental behavior he tries to discover who he is, to establish his ego. This may be a trying experience for him as well as for his parents.

The pastor's role as counselor often requires that he be an interpreter of the adolescent to the parents, who might have felt quite competent to cope with their children when they were young but feel threatened by a being they can no longer control as a child nor understand as an adult.

Usually the counseling emerges from a crisis where the threatened parent has asserted his authority, perhaps in anger, and has been greeted by a defiance he could not manage. As a result the relationship reaches an impasse. The punitive method no longer seems to work in the face of the adolescent's declaration of independence, and the adults who have been used to the role of dignified authority have not had a chance to learn a new way of acting toward this full-sized being who shares the house with them but no longer seems to know what his rightful place in that house should be.

Much pastoral counseling emerges from situational factors that precipitate emotions that are hard to accept. This can be compounded when the emotions are amplified by what we call "normal neuroses." These are times of unusual stress due often to glandular change. Though they usually are worked through in time, they can produce turbulence in the process. When we have the normal stresses of adolescence compounded by the involutional stresses of parents, the need for counseling to restore some balance and perspective to the relationship is apparent.

The following encounter shows some of these forces at work and indicates how in this instance the pastor was an instrument to help bring understanding into a relationship between an adolescent and her parents.

The Emersons were a well-to-do family, proud of their status in the community. Mr. Emerson held a prominent place in local industry, finance and social life. He like to think of himself as perceptive, competent and wise. His wife was more highly emotional but also was quite sure that she was a rather superior person.

Mrs. Emerson initiated the counseling relationship by a phone call requesting a chance to "talk together about something that has upset us considerably."

The Emersons entered my study with an attitude quite different from that which usually characterized them. It found verbal expression in Mrs. Emerson's opening comment: "I never thought we would be coming to our minister with a family problem. We always try to solve our own problems and up till now we have done pretty well with them. But we've got something now that we can't handle. So here we are."

Almost apologetically Mr. Emerson interjected, "What I think Martha is trying to say is that a matter has come up that we would like your advice on, because we are not quite sure that we are proceeding properly. Actually we have not had much experience with such things, so we want to do what is wise and proper for all concerned. That's why we have come to see you."

Everything they had said so far expressed their concern and rather intense emotion, but it had all been general rather than specific. It seemed difficult for them to speak clearly, so I tried to make it easier for them. "I can sense your concern and your wisdom in seeking to talk through your problem, " I said. "But I don't know what it is that you want to talk about."

"Oh, it's about Susan," Mrs. Emerson blurted out as if to immediately stop me from imagining anything else.

"Yes, it's about Susan," Mrs. Emerson echoed. "She hasn't been acting normally of late. We've had an awful time trying to get her to do what she should do, and we've read enough to know what the symptoms of mental illness are. We think she's sick, on the verge of a breakdown, and we'd like to have her put in the right kind of a sanitorium so that she could get help, and come out of this thing without doing herself or anyone else any damage. We thought you might know some good sanitorium where we could put her. Private, of course—we don't want this noised about. It's bad enough to have something like this happen without everyone knowing about it."

Susan was seventeen and a senior in high school. She was a large girl and rather self-conscious about her size. She was an excellent student, elected to the national honor society in her junior year. She tended to be serious, quiet and not too active in social affairs of the school or community. She was chairman of the community relations committee of the youth fellowship and took that task seriously. She had arranged meetings for the fellowship that considered race relations, housing and the plight of the underprivileged in the suburban community where she lived. This interest had embarrassed her family, but they had done nothing more than to suggest that it might be more useful for the young people to keep closer to religious subjects. Also Susan had a thyroid condition, which was being treated by medication, but still she was obviously overweight. I knew Susan quite well, had worked with her in youth programs, had observed her in many different settings and had never detected anything that I felt was abnormal in her behavior.

I felt it was important for the Emersons to examine more fully their decision to commit their daughter to a sanitorium for the treatment of mental illness. I was concerned about the consequences for both Susan and her parents. With these things in mind, I said: "I can appreciate your concern about Susan. She is a girl with fine qualities and great potential. I know you want to protect these things. But this is at least in part a medical problem and what amounts to commitment to an institution would be done under medical supervision. Have you consulted a physician?"

"We know that," Mr. Emerson said with what I assumed was a bit of irritation. "We have not talked with a doctor yet, but we feel sure that that can be arranged. We do not see this as a medical problem as much as a problem of behavior. Whatever we do will be for Susan's best interests, you can be sure."

This last comment showed a determination to take action against Susan that was so explicit that it showed almost a punitive quality. Her behavior had become intolerable, so parental action was being taken against her. But it was also quite obvious that her parents did not interpret their action in those terms, for they felt they were taking reasonable steps in her best interests. I was about to direct comment toward the "problem of behavior" when Mrs. Emerson stepped in with her elaboration on the type of behavior that was distressing them.

"If you had to live with her you would know what we mean by a behavior problem. We have read about behavior disorders, and this is one, right out of the book. She is impossible to live with. Whatever we say she does just the opposite. She deliberately flounts our authority. We try to arrange for her to be with the better type of young people, but what does she do? She hangs around with those hoodlums who wear leather jackets, high boots and ride on motor scooters. We have forbidden her to meet these disreputable characters, but she goes right on doing it. I ride past the high school at noontime, and there she is with them, and when I face her with it she gets sulky and won't even give me a civil answer."

The quality of frustration and anger in her voice as it became more and more high-pitched evidently distressed Mr. Emerson, for he broke into the conversation in a quiet and obviously self-controlled tone of voice: "It's not only that, but we have a medical problem with Susan. She has a gland problem. We have medicine that she is supposed to take carefully. If she takes too much it puts a strain on her heart, and the doctor limits her to three a day. This helps control her weight. But she is not supposed to eat any candy, because she puts on weight so fast. The maid found a whole batch of candy wrappers in her wastebasket, and she used a whole bottle of a hundred pills in a week. This must stop. She knows better, but we can't reason with her. I think she has no self-respect. She looks so sloppy. We are actually ashamed of how she looks, but she doesn't seem to care. I enrolled her in a modeling course. It cost two hundred dollars and has all kinds of training in how to act and walk and wear clothes. It gives rules for diet control—but what happens? She goes a few times and then drops out and I get no refund."

Though Mr. Emerson had started out in a calm voice and was making a strenuous effort to be rational, he became caught up in his emotion. His frustration at not being able to make his daughter into a model was quite clear, and by the time he ended his complaints his voice was showing considerable emotion. Both parents were wrought up by their daughter's behavior and had become so frustrated that they were ready to turn the problem over to an institution. I was getting ready to raise the question of the meaning of Susan's behavior from her point of view when Mrs. Emerson started in again with about the same intensity of feeling and tone quality that she had shown before:

"You have no idea what it is to live in the same house with this sullen person. She disrupts everything. The other children are so well behaved and polite that we can be proud of them, but Susan is insolent, curt and actually revolting to see. She is changing the

whole flavor of our home. We feel we have to protect the rights
of the rest of the family. If she could get the treatment she needs
it would do her good at the same time that we could begin to live
normally again."

Taking advantage of a brief lull, I tried to direct the thinking
toward the meaning of Susan's behavior. I asked, "Don't you
think it would be wise to examine Susan's behavior from her
point of view before deciding what it means?" But the question
was completely ignored by Mr. Emerson, who started speaking
again:

"What you don't seem to see, pastor, is that this problem has
lots of angles. Dr. Philipps (a college professor) is one of the persons we were going to ask to write a recommendation for Susan
at Granville College. He was at the house last Sunday, and Susan actually insulted him. She treats our friends like dirt. We
are so uncomfortable that we don't want to invite people in for
fear she will put on one of her disgraceful acts. You just can't
imagine what it is like unless you see it. It is mortifying."

It was quite clear that the Emersons had been hurt and
angered by their daughter's behavior, but I felt that perhaps
they had expressed enough of their feeling to be ready to start
thinking about the meaning of Susan's behavior and their response to it. So I went back to the question that had been ignored a few minutes earlier. I said, "What do you think Susan is
trying to say through her behavior?"

This thought seemed to puzzle the Emersons. They looked at
each other as if to offer the other a chance to give an answer. As
the pause lengthened it was quite obvious that they were beginning to think along a different line. Finally Mr. Emerson said
quite candidly, "I don't know. I guess we haven't thought much
about it."

"This may be most important for us to think about," I said.
"Up to this point we have considered your reactions to what she
was doing. But it is her behavior that is the point of issue. We
want to find out what it means to her. She isn't here to speak for
herself, so perhaps I could stand in for her. How would it be with
you if I took the behavior you have described and tried to see it

from her point of view. I may not be accurate in my interpretation of it, but at least it will give us a starting point in trying to understand what it means. Is this all right with you?"

The Emersons looked at each other questioningly, as if suspicious of this new turn of the conversation. Mr. Emerson finally said rather resistantly, "Well, that wasn't exactly what we came for, but go ahead anyway."

I started in: "Adolescents are a strange mixture. They are part adult and part child. They want to be independent, but they know they are dependent. They want to be themselves but are not quite sure who they are. They want to experiment with their behavior but run the risk of having their experiments misunderstood. They have strong feelings and limited experience to give them structure. They often appear to be inconsistent, not very reasonable and hard to cope with."

At these words the Emersons seemed to be more comfortable. They looked at each other approvingly, and Mrs. Emerson said, "That sure fits Susan to a T."

"This behavior you describe could well be quite normal for a person going through the glandular change, the emotional stress and the social pressures of adolescence," I resumed. "It is a period of normal neurosis, temporary in nature, but showing itself primarily in difficulties in getting along with other people." The Emersons were paying close attention.

Then I said: "Now let's take the behavior you describe and assume that I am asking Susan what it means, and I will try to give an answer that would make sense to her. First, what about her choice of friends? To this Susan might very well say that she feels embarrassed by all the obvious efforts to set up social contacts for her. She would rather have friends of her own that value her for what she is rather than those who condescend to be nice to her just because of social obligations to her parents. And about the diet and the modeling course? Susan might well say that being on a diet is no fun when all the other kids eat anything. She didn't like the modeling because it was all so superficial. She didn't feel at home there, because those people all wanted something out of life so different from what she wanted. She liked to study and read, and when she read she enjoyed eat-ing. It was her body and her heart. When she ate a lot of candy she took extra pills to help burn up the fat, but she didn't see that it was anybody's concern but hers. Why make a capital offense of it? Nothing she did was appreciated. What the other children did was held up as an example, but they were young kids. They didn't know what it was like to be out of things at school. She got tired of being nagged at all the time about how she looked and what she did. Couldn't people just leave her alone for a while? She was having enough trouble inside of herself without being jumped on at every turn by people who didn't seem to understand what she was going through. And she might end up by saying that she thinks her parents are more interested in their old status than they are in her. But she is determined to be herself no matter how it hurts."

I wondered what the reaction would be to this effort to speak from Susan's point of view. Mrs. Emerson started sputtering but never got a full or coherent sentence out. Mr. Emerson did better: "I think I see what you are driving at, pastor. This is worth thinking about. You know, you really put it to us there. But it makes sense. But we have to live with this, so we are more interested in practical solutions than we are in theories."

The resistance of the last comment was not as strenuous as I had expected. So I felt it was worth accepting it as a basis for my next comment. I said: "That's right. What makes sense is in the long run usually most practical. When our thinking gets bogged down in our strong feelings, we may say and do things that are quite impractical. This I am quite sure you would not want to do; otherwise you would not have come to talk things over with me. It is important to examine Susan's behavior at home, at school and in the church, for it is all a part of her and it all fits together to give us a more accurate picture of what is going on in her. I was speaking of her as I see her. That is but a part. You speak as you know her, and that too is a part. Her school record is another part . . ."

Here Mrs. Emerson broke in: "Well, that at least is something we can be proud of. The reports from school are always excellent. It is at home that we have the most trouble."

I felt this was worth more consideration as a basis for more objectivity, so I said: "You speak of most of the trouble being at home. What do you think that means?"

Mrs. Emerson answered quickly: "Why, naturally we are the ones who have to be responsible for her and that's where the run-ins come. If we just left her alone everything would be all right, but we can't do that. We are her parents. We can't just let things go by unnoticed. We have to make sure that she turns out all right."

"Yes, I know," I said. "But what do you think would happen if Susan were taken out of school and committed to a sanitorium to associate with a number of seriously disturbed persons?"

"But we were thinking of a high-grade place with only the best environment," said Mr. Emerson. "Really, that is what we had come to talk with you about. We thought you might know of a place like that under church auspices."

"That is another matter, really. But the question I raised seems to warrant consideration first. What would this do to Susan?"

"Well, we hoped it would be good for her and that she would come around in time to understand that it was for her good. As parents we have to make unpleasant choices sometimes. And we were thinking about the rest of the family too," Mr. Emerson answered.

The resistance and the efforts to divert the consideration of the question was quite obvious. But probably the focal point of consideration was also here. So I said again, "Because Susan has no chance to speak for herself, I keep stressing that we need to consider the meaning of her behavior and what the meaning of your plan of action would be for her. What you suggest is, I think you will admit, rather drastic. I sense the threat that her behavior creates for you, but I also feel it would not be wise to deal with it punitively. She is a sensitive person going through a difficult period of adjustment, and she needs the help that makes it possible for her to value herself, grow in respect and confidence. She will be going to college in a few months. These next few months will be important for her. They will be the last months when you will have her as a member of the household, for after she gets to college she will probably be home only for visits."

Mr. Emerson responded, "It is clear you don't think much of our plan. I'm beginning to see why. But we have to do something. What do you suggest?"

"Really, it is not my function to suggest specific plans of action," I said. "But I may be able to be useful in helping you see what some of the alternatives can be, so that when you make your decisions you will be able to do it more objectively. And I think I have given some of the bases for this objectivity as we have moved along."

"You mean trying to see Susan's side of things for a change, and being more patient?" Mr. Emerson asked.

"Yes, it's partly that," I said. "But don't you think it is important to try to understand why this whole matter has upset you so? It is the first time your parental authority has been challenged, and it is quite an adjustment to recognize that there is another person in the house struggling to assert her will. This becomes quite a test of love, and usually people need love the most when they seem to warrant it the least."

"Well, if you haven't done anything else you have helped us stand off and look at this from a new angle." Mr. Emerson's hostility was still evident, but it was directed more at me than at Susan now, which was probably all to the good.

I had moved more directly than usual in this interview for the simple reason that their minds had already been made up on a course of action that could have been unwise and destructive. I had to raise issues that challenged it in a limited time. I had to recognize the strong feelings present and accept some of the threat they presented. The interview ended with an invitation for the Emersons to participate in a revolving group therapy session for parents of adolescents. This they agreed to do. They also had a talk with the school psychologist who assured them that Susan was functioning well within normal bounds for her age.

When Susan left for college the family was strengthened by its experience for dealing constructively with the declaration of independence of the next adolescent. Several times the Emersons recalled our conversation and commented, "You certainly saved us from making a terrible mistake."

Chapter 23

"I Don't Get Anything Out of Your Sermons"

A defensive stance is usually a weak point to start from in establishing constructive conversation. It is not uncommon for people to come to the pastor to voice some criticism. If the pastor becomes defensive he is apt to lost contact with the counselee. He may fail to use an important opportunity for growth.

In the following encounter a person with quite a different social and religious orientation came to the pastor with strong criticism. The pastor moved beyond the criticism to try to understand its meaning in the life of the individual. The man's speech and body language spoke volumes. He assessed the situation as one that would not be affected by subtlety or indirection. So the pastor was direct but not defensive. He was conciliatory but not inclined to abandon his concern for a needed form of human growth.

The Sunday morning service was over. Most of the people had gone. The pastor greeted the last few members of the congregation and noticed one of the newer members of the parish standing off to one side. When everyone else had gone, Mr. Harris came over to the pastor and said, "Good morning, preacher. Got any time for an old sinner like me?"

The pastor responded, "Sure thing, Mr. Harris. What's on your mind?"

"Well, I might as well be frank," Mr. Harris began. "When we moved up here we thought being as it was the same kind of church we'd get the same kind of preaching. Now, I'm not saying that you're not smart enough, or anything like that, because I guess you are. But I never once heard you talk about Hell or punishment. You act like you never heard about sin and salvation. I sometimes wonder if you're really a saved-and-born-again Christian."

"Sounds like we've got lots of things to talk about. Let's go inside where the sun's not so hot. How about sitting here in the back pew? Now, I gather you're disappointed in the kind of religion we preach here. Am I right?"

"Right on. I don't think your kind of preaching could ever do anyone any good. You don't tell any of the old Bible stories. You don't talk about damnation. You don't threaten with everlasting punishment. How do you ever expect to convert sinners if you don't give them the true Bible message?" Mr. Harris complained.

The pastor listened intently and said, "How do you think it should be done?"

"Well, man, you can't just talk to people like they weren't sinners. Take me, man. I need help to fight the Devil every day of my life. I'm not getting any help from you. We've been coming here for three months, and I haven't gotten any help in fighting the good fight. If I don't get some help soon I'm going someplace where they preach the Gospel. And you know I don't want to do that, because the wife and kids like it here, but I'll drag them all out, if I need to. Because salvation's that important to me," Mr. Harris said.

"Mr. Harris," the pastor responded, "I believe you have had an experience of salvation. Would you like to tell me about it?"

"I sure would," said Mr. Harris. "I'm never tired of givin' my testimony. I remember just the time and place. It was like lightning struck. The Holy Spirit came down and flooded my life, and I'm a new man in Christ ever since. It was in the Birmingham Avenue Church. It was November 25th. I'll never forget it. The preacher talked on sin and he got me under conviction. I shook like a leaf under the power of the spirit. I went to the altar and he prayed with me and I got up a new man. I got the upper hand on the Devil and, man, I want to keep it that way."

"That's a remarkable story," the pastor said. "It must have been an important turning point in your life. Do you want to tell me more about it—your background, I mean, your former life?"

"I sure do. Praise the good Lord. My papa was a power of the spirit preacher. He was a good man but very strict. He said the Lord appointed him to guide his people. Our family, all nine of us, were scared of the vengeance of the Lord. There was no sass in our home. I saw my papa wallop my brother right across the room. When the good Lord told him to do something he did it. I saw him twist my mama's hair until she repented. He was a real Christian and people feared the wrath of the Lord when he was under the Spirit."

The pastor nodded to Mr. Harris to go on.

Mr. Harris continued: "When I was fifteen I joined the navy —had to lie about my age a little. Not much. Then when I did my stint I worked in the oil rigs and steel mills. Always in trouble—drinking and fighting and women. I was a sinner, the worst sinner on earth, I'm sure. But the Lord, He was laying for me. I followed a pretty young thing to church. You see, the Lord was baiting the trap. And then He sprung it and I was under the conviction. I tell you, I had the terrors and I shook like a leaf. The Lord was getting to me. And when the good Lord strikes, man, you are helpless. Like the Good Book says, I was the clay and He was the potter. I was made a new man. And I plan to stay that way."

The pastor listened intently. "So the Lord opened up a new life to you, and you want to keep this new life."

"That's it. Exactly. And you are not helping the Lord one bit. That's what I'm trying to tell you. You aren't helping one bit. That's your job, and you aren't doing it."

"Yes, Mr. Harris, you're making your point well, but I'm not quite sure you have made clear what you want me to do about it."

"Do? Why, man—preach the Gospel. Talk about sin. Make me so ashamed of my sin I'll never do it again," Mr. Harris pleaded.

"Why? Do you still feel like sinning?"

"Man, is the Devil working hard on me. Every day. Every hour. Every minute. I'm saved and I'm beyond committing sin, but the old Devil he never gives up. I was one of his favorites for years, and he doesn't want to let go. He is struggling for my soul, and God is so busy with other people that He isn't always right there. That's where you come in. You've got to be there to help me with the Devil. If you scare the Devil enough on Sunday, I can get through the week. But if you don't, man, I'm in real danger. See what I mean?"

"Yes, I see what you mean. And I want to help you. I hope you believe that," the pastor said. "And I think I have something very good to offer you if you'll consider it. Do you remember the woman at the well in Samaria that Jesus talked with one day? She was apparently a deeply troubled woman who had lived a sinful life. But did Jesus talk with her about her sin or the Devil or other things of that sort? No, he did something better. He offered her a spring of water within that would spring up to guarantee the security of her spirit. Do you remember that story?"

"Sure. I read my Bible," Mr. Harris said.

"I'm sure you do, so you will understand what I am trying to say. There is an external kind of salvation, like the external water which has to be continually renewed. But there is another kind that comes from within that is so sure that you never have to worry again about losing control of yourself. You will no longer have this constant battle going on inside of you between the Devil and the Lord, as you speak of it."

Mr. Harris didn't seem convinced.

The pastor continued: "You have said yourself that you are in constant need of help from outside—me, or some other preacher, to scare the Devil out of you for a few days, otherwise you might suffer a relapse. Is that right?"

"Yes, man. I don't want to be no backslider. I don't want my feet in slippery places."

"What I would like to help you do is find that security within yourself that is so great that you will never again feel threatened. You will then be not only a born-again Christian but you will also be a grown-up, a mature Christian who can stand on his own two feet without help from anyone. You will be in right relation with God. You will know the inner skills that will make your salvation complete."

"You mean my salvation ain't complete?" Mr. Harris asked angrily. "You have no right to say that."

"I didn't say that, if you remember. *You* said it. You said the Devil was struggling for your soul. You said you needed help every hour. I'm saying that I think you can find a way to live without this constant fear, this everlasting battle inside of you. You can go off looking for another preacher who will try to scare the Devil out of you, but that will only prolong your inner battle. You may get some help, but it will only be temporary. I would like to help you find what Jesus offered the woman at the well in Samaria, a new discovery of the spiritual resources in yourself, a new inner strength that will be sufficient for all of your needs. That is the kind of religion I try to preach. It may be new to you, but it comes right out of the Bible. I'd like to share it with you, if you'll let me."

"You're sure it comes right out of the Bible?" Mr. Harris asked.

"I take it that you ran away from home because you could not stand the fear and terror you felt there. You ran away and did all of the things your father would have punished you for. But you never felt good about it and went back to a preacher who talked like your father to make some kind of peace within yourself." The pastor watched the surprised look on Mr. Harris's face and asked, "Isn't that so?"

"How'd you know that?" Mr. Harris seemed incredulous.

"You told me, remember? You were troubled about what happened to your brother and your mother, but you didn't dare admit it for fear of your father, so you had to run away and join the navy. But that wasn't good enough, was it? Even the salvation you finally gained was not a mature and complete thing. It was like a boy going back to ask his father's forgiveness because he wasn't really sure of himself yet."

The pastor continued: "In a way you've been carrying your father around inside of you all these years. You have been asking me to become your threatening father again. But I wouldn't want to do that, because I think you are ready for something better. You can free yourself from that terrorizing past. You can discover a God of love who will help you discover your own strength and help you win a victory inside of yourself, so that you'll never need me or anyone else to join your inner battle."

Mr. Harris sat a long while, as if deep in thought. The pastor watched to see if his last few comments had been more than Mr. Harris could take.

Finally Mr. Harris looked up and said: "You know, man, there's some truth to what you say. I treat my kids and my old woman the way my father did, and I always feel kind of sick inside when I do. But I can't seem to stop myself. I guess I never knew much about love and that stuff."

Again there was quite a long period of silence. Then Mr. Harris said, "Maybe I'll be back to church next Sunday."

The pastor said he hoped so and added, "You know, I think lots of good things can happen to people when they sit and talk like we've been doing. I spend a lot of time each week just talking with people the way I think Jesus must have done with people in His day, about their problems and their thoughts and feelings. Any time you want to just sit and talk like we've been doing, I'd be glad to do it. I think that is one of the ways we discover the strength we have inside."

Mr. Harris mused: "You know, I never sat and talked with anyone like this. I argue and fight a lot with people, but never just talk about deep things like this. Sure, I'd like to talk some more. It kind of makes you feel good inside, doesn't it, to know you can talk without fighting."

Often aggressive persons come to their pastor to work off some of their anger. They may not even know the meaning of their behavior, and the pastor may never have occasion to tell them. But in his encounter with them he can help them grow into larger perspectives and healthier attitudes toward themselves and others. Here again a defensive stance would destroy the chance for exploration and growth. It might almost be a maxim for constant use that, when a person comes with criticism or expressions of hostility, it is a time to be alert to what lies behind it. If we work on the principle that all behavior is meaningful, we do not take behavior too personally but rather search out what the behavior is saying beyond the words that are uttered. The many-faceted relationship that the pastor has with his people in the parish multiplies his chances to observe and respond to meaningful behavior. The process is never-ending, and his privileged status grows with use.

Chapter 24

Jealousy and a Fear of Christmas

Most pastors have observed that the number of persons seeking advice and counsel about emotional problems tend to increase at the time of family holidays and the weeks that follow them. Many of the deepest emotional problems are related to feelings toward parents and sibling rivalries. These are increased at times of family reunion the holiday periods make possible.

Often persons are baffled and confused by the feelings that seem so inappropriate and out of keeping with the season. They open reservoirs of emotion that they have quite well closed off during the rest of the year. The more intense the emotions surrounding the experience, the more baffling may be the feelings that they contend with.

The following pastoral relationship grew out of a holiday emotion with deep roots in childhood and also the frustrations of adult life. Because of the readiness of the person to act, the counseling process moved rapidly.

"I am so glad you could see me right away. I feel something terrible coming on, and I don't know how to cope with it. It has been growing for several years, and last year I was determined to do something about it, and I did, but it wasn't the right thing. This year I am determined to face it or I am sure it will break me."

So it was that Mildred M. started our interview. She was quite sure she knew what she was talking about. I had to wait to find out. But that she was distressed and felt a crisis approaching was quite clear. I felt I had to be very careful in leading her into an elaboration, for she had so carefully avoided saying what it was she could not cope with. So I said, "Do you want to tell me more precisely what it is you are apprehensive about?"

"I am afraid that if I tell you you will laugh at me, for it seems like the craziest thing you have ever heard of. That is what makes it so difficult for me. No one could possibly imagine how I feel or why. I can't myself, but I know I do. Oh, please don't laugh at me if I tell you. That would be the last straw." Tears were in her eyes as she made that last plea.

"You may be sure that I am concerned about your feelings, and I certainly don't think it is a laughing matter to be as upset as you are," I reassured her.

"I know how strange it must sound to you, but it is the simple fact. I am frightened out of my wits by Christmas and Santa Claus. I have tried to control it, but I can't. This time of year is unbearable. Everyone else is having such a wonderful time, and the more fun they have the more isolated I become. I go home from work by back streets because they are not decorated so much. I lock myself in my apartment and play records and read all evening. If I turn on the radio or TV, I can't stand it. It's just more and more Christmas. I know I should love the festival of Christ's birth, but I hate it. I want to get away as far as possible. Why do people have to rub it in for weeks and months?" She paused for a moment and then went on when I failed to answer what I thought was a rhetorical question. "Last year I thought I might outwit the awful feeling so I went to the office party. I never drink, but they had a big bowl of punch and I took a couple of drinks and it was spiked. I felt warm and relaxed, the first time I had felt that way since before Thanksgiving. I took another and another, and they must have taken me home. I don't remember. But I knew something had made me feel good for a little while. I stopped at a liquor store next day and bought some sherry. I just know I couldn't get through this season without it, but I don't want to be that way. There must be something I could do to beat this terrible feeling before I make myself into an alcoholic. I can't even go to church this time of year, for the church is just dripping Christmas. Don't you understand what it is like? Can't you do anything to help me? Oh, I am sure no one has ever had a problem like this." She put her hands to her face and shook with sobs.

Mildred was a member of the Business and Professional Women's Group in the parish. She had come to the city several years back and had worked as a research chemist for a large firm. She always gave the appearance of self-assured competence, and though I saw her often in group activity I had never gotten well enough acquainted to know her background or personality traits. However, her outpouring of feeling appeared to be out of character as I had observed her. It seemed that the cause-effect relationships were out of proportion. This is often the clue to an anxiety state where some circumstance triggers a pent-up reservoir of emotion and it pours out disproportionately. This appeared to be the case with Mildred. Usually the anxiety is centered upon a threat to the integrity of being. The threats attach themselves to an event or a person, in this case Christmas and the symbolic person, Santa. The threats are usually diffused fears that may be dealt with more adequately if they are brought into focus. The task then is to help make the generalized more specific, in effect change the diffused anxiety into real fears that can at least be recognized for what they are. Then, perchance, something can be done about them.

I felt that it was important for Mildred to talk about her fears for two reasons. She might reveal to me some clues as to the causes that led to the effects, and in her verbalization she might reveal something to herself that was significant. At the least she might relieve the stress from the feelings she held in at some considerable personal discomfort. So I said: "Yes, I understand how painful your anxiety must be. I am quite sure something can be done to help relieve it. But I am also sure that we will want to explore this feeling and its cause-effect relationships more. Can you remember anything about what happened when you were first aware of these feelings?"

She thought awhile and then said: "Yes, I remember quite well when I first felt some of these feelings. It was several years ago. One of the girls I had worked with invited me to have dinner with her family on Christmas Eve. It was all quite lighthearted and gay. We had a good meal. We told the children stories, and they climbed all over me. She has three children, five, three and one. Nothing was said, but I had the feeling she was trying to be nice to me because she had so much and I had so little. I felt she was parading her husband, her children, her home, her Christmas Eve. As the evening went on, the children were put to bed and we all pitched in to decorate the tree. They kept talking about the children in the morning, their eyes, the film for the camera, the stockings and the presents. Like a shot it hit me that their kindness was the worst kind of cruelty. I made some excuse to leave and went back to my apartment. I had a wooden bowl full of cards I had received. When I took off my coat, the first thing I did was throw that bowl against the wall. The cards went all over. The bowl broke. I got down on my knees and picked up the cards. I got some glue and mended the bowl. Then I just sat there and wondered what had happened to me. I never did things like that. Well, I guess that is the beginning of things. Every year since then it has seemed like more of an ordeal."

While she talked she was quite spontaneous. After the last sentence she paused, as if her spontaneity had run out. It seemed to me that this episode had merely triggered her major emotional concern about her unmarried status. But nothing she had said showed that she had made any such connection, so I felt she was not ready to approach that idea. So I made a generalized statement about Christmas and emotion, wondering where she might move with it. I said: "Christmas produces strong feelings, especially with children. Or children can precipitate it in adults. Some of our earliest memories cluster about Christmas events. Often they are unexamined memories. What were Christmases like when you were a child?"

"It's strange that you should ask that," she said, looking at me quizzically. "Just before I came over here I recalled something that set me to thinking. In fact it upset me so much, I decided then that I would have to talk with somebody."

Then she stopped as if she were hesitant to go ahead with the painful recollection. I didn't say anything, but I looked as if I were expecting her to continue.

Finally she went on: "I didn't have too pleasant a childhood. My father was a truck driver. He worked hard and he drank hard. It was difficult for my mother. When he came home at night, we never knew what to expect. Mother was always frightened, I am sure. When he would stamp his feet on the porch, she would say, 'Here comes your father,' and we would all run and hide. I remember I had a favorite place, under a side table in the dining room. From there I could watch him come in. We could never be sure of his mood. He might be angry and cursing, and sometimes he beat my mother brutally. At other times he might be very affectionate and pick her up off her feet (she was a little thing), and swing her around and pretend he was dancing. Either way it was frightening to me. Sometimes she would cry and sometimes laugh. But from where I hid I couldn't tell the difference." She stopped as if to see how I was taking it.

I said, "I can see how difficult that must have been, and then . . ."

"Well, as I was starting to tell you," she continued, "it was the thing I recalled about Christmas Eve. I think I was four. It was dark. We heard stamping feet on the porch and then a knocking on the window. My mother called, 'Come and see Santa.' I came from my hiding place and there, looking through the window, was a hideous face. My father must have bought a cheap mask and red hat. At any rate he looked frightful to me. I began to cry and ran to my mother. She tried to comfort me and said, 'Don't cry. That is your father playing Santa.' Then he came in and took off his mask and I was just as frightened. I ran and hid in my favorite place, and he came and pulled me out and laughed at me as if it were great sport. I tried to get away from him and he chased me. I ran around a table and hit my head on it. It began to bleed. My father got angry, and my mother tried to comfort me and clean up the mess. There were words about 'stupid kids you couldn't play with.' All in all it was a terrible evening, and I guess I have never gotten over it."

It was quite obvious she had exposed some traumatic material that had many ramifications. I did not know how much interpretation she had given to the material, but her last comment implied that she was ready to explore some of the meanings. So I said, "You feel you haven't gotten over it. How do you mean?"

"I don't really know," she started. "I just try to run away from it, like I did then."

This could have been moving toward real insight, but it was not clear yet just what she meant, so I asked, "Running away? How so?"

"Oh, don't you see?" She seemed quite excited now. "I have always been afraid of my father. I seldom go home. He has quieted down now that he is older, but I always see him from under the table. I pity my mother, but I really think I hate my father. It's terrible to hate your own father."

I decided to restate her last idea more sharply. "You don't go home because you are still running away from your father. Santa represents father, so you run away from it too, is that it?"

At first she wasn't ready to go along with the idea. She sat quietly for a while. Then she said, "I suppose so."

I assumed I had moved too rapidly, so I backed off a bit and sat quietly for a while as if I too were thinking with her. Then I said: "Perhaps you don't hate your father as much as you think. No, as an adult, you may be trying to understand more about him than you did as a child. Could that be a possibility?"

"I don't know how you get that idea," she snapped back.

"I have been trying to understand something you did. When your emotional problem became intolerable you turned to alcohol, even though you had unpleasant childhood memories connected with it. Was this an effort to identify with your father as a real person with real problems that he tried to solve in that way?" I watched closely to see how she responded to this suggestion.

"You know, I never thought of that. I wondered myself why I would do such a thing. You know, I never thought of that." She was pensive.

Then for a while she talked about her father, the confused pattern of his living, his brusque exterior and signs of tenderness. She became almost completely absorbed in the subject. As if it were a long-postponed task, she talked about this man as if he were a person, rather than a frightening image. It seemed that she was quite comfortable in talking about him. She related many other incidents that came from her childhood and youth that began to fill in the picture of a troubled but entirely human character. She ended her long discourse by saying, "You know, I have never talked like this about my father in my whole life."

Now that insight seemed to be coming in large chunks, I went on with the exploration. I asked, "Do you see any connection between the evening with your friend and that earlier Christmas Eve?"

"Yes," she said and sat quite a while thinking.

Then she started in on her own feelings about her life. She said she felt cheated of so much. She wanted to be like other women but never seemed able to be. She admitted that she was afraid of men and was always afraid that she would be hurt. In protecting herself she also deprived herself. She poured out events that illustrated this contradiction in her whole way of life. She ended this self-revelation by saying, "The older I get the more I feel that I am getting lost in a world of my fears and may never get out."

I wanted to pull some things together in her thinking so I asked: "How do you feel, talking about all of these things?"

"Oh, I feel so relieved. You know, having someone to talk to brought out a lot of things I had never thought of in the same way before. I don't have to let that early experience plague me all the rest of my life." She looked at me as if she were going to make a startling statement. "You know, I think I am going home for Christmas, I have found some excuse for staying away for years, but now I think it will be different. Maybe I can see my father like a person—not from under the table."

Facing an emotion and talking about it freely brings a new perspective. Much unfinished business of childhood plagues persons through life. The chance to see parents as people is often a first step toward this new maturity. The more heightened the emotional content of an experience, the more difficult it may be to get to the point where something constructive can be done about it. Perhaps this is why so much disillusionment, frustration and unreasonable behavior attached themselves to the Christmas season.

As far as Mildred was concerned, there had been so much morbid material in her consciousness, and it had been so repressed, that it seemed the unfinished business of her emotional growth had to be considered further. Not only was the door kept open for further conversation, but the pastor assessed the need for referral to get at some of the deeper problems that might have to do with her anxiety, her attitude toward herself and her feelings about marriage.

Chapter 25

"Should I Tell Him How Sick He Is?"

Much of the pastor's time is spent with those who are sick in a hospital. Often questions arise as to how members of the family should proceed in their relations with the sick. The pastor is an accessible resource for talking over the problems.

Usually it is wise in the hospital setting for the pastor to be familiar with hospital procedures and personnel. He should work in cooperation with them and be responsive to their ways of operating. But he should also realize that there are times when physicians might want to thrust some of their responsibilities on others. This may mean that the pastor is placed in a position where he must help a family member think through his role in talking about difficult subjects.

It is always important for the pastor to find out as much as he can about the circumstances involved as well as the emotional conditions of the persons concerned. His opinion should be held in abeyance, and his efforts should be directed toward helping others to arrive at behavior they would be comfortable with over a long period of time.

The following encounter is quite typical. The pastor gave little direct suggestion but employed the simple idea of role-playing to bring some feelings into focus. It seemed that Mrs. Santone knew what she wanted to do and felt right about doing it but was unable to find the ways for doing it. The pastor assessed his role as that of helping her find the ways for doing what she needed to do.

The pastor had called on Mr. Santone at the hospital. The conversation was general and nothing was said about the nature or seriousness of Mr. Santone's ailment. Mrs. Santone was also in the room during the pastor's visit and shared in the conversation.

When the pastor left she followed him out of the room and down the corridor a way until they were well out of earshot of the patient's room. Then quite bluntly she said, "Do you think we should tell him how sick he is?"

The pastor suggested that they go to the family room at the end of the hallway and sit down for a while. When they were seated the pastor rephrased her question, "So you are wondering if you should tell your husband how sick he is. How do you mean that, Mrs. Santone?"

"The doctor told me he will not get well. He wouldn't say how long, but probably just a few weeks. He said it would probably be best not to say anything to him about it but that he couldn't tell me what to say or not to say. It's cancer in several places and spreading all the time," Mrs. Santone explained.

"So the doctor left the final decision up to you. How do you feel about it?" the pastor asked.

"I don't think I should have to decide. I don't know enough about all the things involved. I want to do what is good for him. But how am I to know that?"

"The doctor knows more about the medical problem, that is sure. But he must have felt you knew more about your husband and how he reacts. He wanted you to have freedom to do the personal and nonmedical things that made sense to you."

"Oh, I know my husband, all right," Mrs. Santone answered. "He is an emotional man. He can get upset and go all to pieces. But he usually gets upset over little things. When it is something big, he seems to do better."

"How do you think he would feel about this?"

Mrs. Santone thought awhile, then said: "Sometimes I think he knows there's something wrong. A couple of times he said, 'You wouldn't lie to me would you?' and I always said, 'You know me, I never did, so why should I start now?' But he doesn't seem satisfied. He's a smart man, you know. I don't think we could really fool him for long."

The pastor listened and watched, and Mrs. Santone continued after a while: "It's the look in his eye that gets me. Always when I go in he looks deep in my eyes for a long time like he was trying to see something there. I try to look him straight in the eye but finally it gets me and I turn away. When I turn back again his look has changed as much as to say, I know so don't try to kid me. But he never comes right out and says it."

"You think he knows but doesn't want to put you on the spot. He thinks you know but don't feel comfortable talking about it. So you play a game with each other," the pastor suggested.

"That's about it," Mrs. Santone said. "But this is no time to play games. We've always told the truth to each other even when it hurts. We've built our life together on the goal of complete honesty and openness. Maybe we haven't always been a hundred per cent, but we always tried. Now it doesn't seem right to play a game, like you say."

"Doing what you think is right is important. There are lots of feelings in all this. When we try to figure out what is right sometimes we have to sort out our feelings."

"That's just it. My feelings get so mixed up. I just want to talk all the time about pleasant things, like the cute things the grandchildren say and do. I want to talk about how the garden is growing. I want to keep everything pleasant and comfortable." Mrs. Santone pondered these thoughts. "But I can't do it, because I'm always thinking he may not see the grandchildren again or he may not see his rose garden. And he loves it so much. So I am mixed up all the time."

"You want to be fair with him?"

"Yes, of course, but what is fair? Should I make his last weeks as carefree and pleasant as possible? Or should I fill them with apprehension and fear of death? Should I help keep him calm, or should I say and do the things that are bound to upset him?"

"Probably what makes you feel mixed up is that you know it isn't as simple as that. Being fair is more than just trying to play games and deceive someone. It calls for something far more basic. It looks at the foundation of the human relationship. These next few weeks may be the most important in your lives for both of you. What is at stake here?"

"Yes, I know you're right. It isn't just a matter of being comfortable and saying the right things. It's how we're going to use the time we have left. But how do you decide?"

The pastor pondered this last question and finally said, "Maybe you could think about reversing roles. Suppose you were in his place. What would you want?"

"Oh, that's no problem. I'd want to know all there is. It's my life. Who has a better right to know?" she responded.

"Why would you want to know?"

"Oh, lots of reasons," she quickly responded. "First, I think I would have a right to know. Then there would be so many things to do. And so little time—I wouldn't have any time to waste."

"Would you think your husband might feel the same way?"

"When you put it that way, I'm sure he does. He is the one who has the right to know. His mind is so alert. He probably doesn't want to waste any valuable time either. I think he should know. But why do you think the doctor thought it would be better if he didn't?"

"You think your husband has the right to know but wonder why the doctor doesn't agree. I suppose we would have to ask the doctor about that. But the fact that he left it up to you modifies his judgment. Apparently he didn't feel it was critical. He left you free to use your own judgment, didn't he?"

"Yes, that's so. But I wonder . . . How can I tell him? What do I say? What should I be prepared for? All of these questions have to be answered."

"With things like this it is not a matter of one right or one wrong way of doing it. There may be many right ways. There are opportunities that come along. There are ways of doing it naturally and gradually. And with help. You don't have to do things all by yourself. And it is probably more important how you do it than that you do it."

Mrs. Santone pondered this for a while and then said, "Suppose the next time he asks about telling him the truth, I just do it then."

"That would be an opportunity. But it would be a matter of how you did it. Maybe it is best to do it together. I mean, let him share in the discovery of the truth about himself as much as possible."

"How would I do that?" she asked.

"Let's say the next time he asks about telling the truth, you respond by asking, 'What are you getting at, dear?' and he might respond, 'I have the uneasy feeling that you are not telling me all you know.' Then you could respond by asking, 'What do you think I am keeping from you?' And in that way you could move toward the subject. You could find out what he is thinking at the same time you are giving him the information you have. It is more a matter of being gentle and open than being blunt and cruel," the pastor responded. "See what I mean?"

"Yes, I suppose so. But what if he doesn't say the things you just suggested. He might say, 'Okay, if it's that bad skip it.' I know him. He might just try to make it easy for me not to go into detail."

"It could be. But if you think it is fair to him to be open and honest, then you move with the conversation as it seems natural at the time. No one can predict what another will say one hundred per cent. Conversations are alive, and they move according to the feelings of the moment. I was suggesting a way you might approach the subject."

"I really feel that we should do it. Since the doctor told me and I have been trying to keep it to myself, I have felt as if a wall was slowly rising between us. I think we would all feel better if the wall was down. I know it won't be easy, but we've always been so close, I think we need each other now. Being honest can be hard, but it's better than being dishonest, even at a time like this," Mrs. Santone thought out loud.

She continued: "You've probably done this many times. Do you think you could help me with it? I'd feel better about it if I thought you would be around to back me up."

The pastor answered: "Of course, I'll help in any way I can. I don't want to intrude on your conversation, but if you think I can add anything by being there and sharing things, I'll surely try. Maybe you want to check with your doctor so that he knows what is happening and you can get his feelings about the matter. Then let me know and I'll plan to be with you."

Several days passed, and Mrs. Santone talked with her doctor and the pastor. When the pastor visited the hospital room, Mrs. Santone was standing by the bed. She said, "We had quite a talk this morning, didn't we, dear? I told you my husband was real smart. He had things pretty well figured out. It has done us so much good just to talk so freely about it all—our feelings—our plans—and the doctor has said that he can come home for a while. We are so happy about that. We know we can face anything together. We're going to make the most of the rest of our life."

While the pastor was willing to be with Mrs. Santone and help her in communicating with her husband, he found when he arrived that she had already talked things over with her husband and they both seemed to feel relieved and comfortable about what they had been able to do. Also it had been possible to bring the physician into their discussion with some plans for using the rest of their time most fruitfully.

Chapter 26

What to Do About Senile Dementia

With the rapid change in social patterns and health care resources, the population of the aged has increased rapidly. Older people may remain in good physical condition comparatively, with deterioration of their mental states. This creates complex problems for their care and for the emotional states of those who feel a responsibility for them. Increasingly there are the forms of anguish related to anticipatory grief. Also there are deep feelings of guilt. Often people struggling with these problems come to their pastor for help.

Such was the case of Mrs. Folsome who made an appointment to talk something over with her pastor.

"I feel like such a criminal," Mrs. Folsome blurted out as soon as she had been seated in her pastor's study. I just hate myself for what I've done. But I just had to do it, so what do I do? How can a person stand herself when she does what she has to do but can't stand doing what she had to do?"

These imprecatory remarks came pouring out with no expla-
nation, and it was quite obvious Mrs. Folsome was upset at herself. But what it was did not show up in the jumble of words that
showed her emotion.

The pastor said, "I'm not quite sure I understand what it is
that is bothering you. Maybe you can clarify things a bit."

Mrs. Folsome continued: "But you should know what it
means to do something you know you shouldn't do even when
you know you have to do it. But to do it to a sweet little person
who trusts you so much and has done so much for you, why that
is inexcusable in my book. It's hard to live with and I'm just not
living with it. That's all. I never knew anything could affect a
person like this. It just has me so upset all of the time that I
can't stand it."

"Yes, Mrs. Folsome," said the pastor. "I sense how upset you
are, but you have not made it clear to me what you have done
that is so distressing."

"You should realize when it is a case like this, that it is impossible to do anything about it," Mrs. Folsome continued. "It
says in the Bible to honor your father and mother, and I don't
want to break one of the Commandments. And when someone
has taken care of you for years and done everything for you like
a mother, it is too cruel not to do the same thing for her when
she is helpless and can't take care of herself anymore. That's
what makes me feel so guilty. I feel I've committed a crime, and
what is the trouble with me is I know it but there wasn't a thing I
could do about it."

"So it is something about your mother," the pastor guessed.

"It certainly is. That poor little old lady who never did a thing
to hurt anybody. She brought up her children and loved them
every one. And also her sister's child after she died. And now it
comes to this. It makes me feel so terrible. I can't stand myself."

The pastor asked: "Could you tell me about your mother,
where she is now and how she is?"

"That's the whole problem," Mrs. Folsome responded. "It's
where she is. To think of that poor little old lady who never did
an unkind thing in her life in a place like that with all those

other people who are so crippled, and drooling and empty-faced. It shouldn't happen to my mother. But I did it myself and I have to take the blame. But she's all right. She is polite and kind. She's easy to get along with. There is really nothing the matter with her, but the doctor said she had to be watched twenty-four hours a day. You see, there is really nothing the matter with her physically, but her mind is affected. She doesn't know what she is doing. She goes out in the cold without a coat and lets the kettles burn out and calls people any hour of the day or night. She looks all right but she just lives in her own world and does things her own way. That's not so wrong is it? She has a right to be herself. She's never hurt anyone, but I've hurt her and I feel so guilty."

"Now let me put things together a bit," the pastor said. "On the advice of your mother's doctor you placed her in a nursing home where she could have constant supervision, and you feel upset about having to do this. Is that right?"

"Well, wouldn't you? If it was your own mother? In with all of those other people who are not like her at all. It is just like putting her in prison. What reward is that for all the good things she has done for people all of her life?" Mrs. Folsome asked.

It began to be obvious that Mrs. Folsome was suffering from the special kind of guilt that has come along with medical advancement and architectural and social change. What was traditionally an accepted fact—that the parents cared for children when they needed it and the children in turn cared for their parents when they became old or helpless—is being overturned. Many persons who can accept the logic of the new ways of coping with old age and deteriorative disease have not yet made the psychological adjustment to these conditions and often need special help in dealing with these emotional problems.

The pastor moved slowly toward the problem. He said: "Yes, it seems like a whole new way of coping with the problems of the aged. There have been so many changes in recent years. One hardly begins . . ."

Mrs. Folsome interrupted: "You know there isn't one of her children that could take care of her. Things have changed. We all live in apartments, you know, with just a few rooms. Then during the day there is no one around because nearly everyone works now. I can remember when an aunt of mine got old she moved in with her younger sister. It was expected. There was a big house and lots of room and always somebody there. When my grandmother was an old lady she came and lived with my father and mother. It was expected. But they had a big house and lots of room. Things are so different now, and it all seems so wrong. Nobody thinks about the old folks. They just get shunted off into these prisons."

"Yes, there are many changes. Some of them are deliberate. Medical skills now control most infectious diseases so that more and more people die of deteriorative diseases. Did the doctor tell you what the diagnosis was of your mother's ailment?" the pastor asked.

"Well, yes. He tried to explain to me what was happening. He said that the arteries in the brain were hardening and that this limited the blood supply and so my mother couldn't think very well. He explained that at eighty-four much of her mind was affected. That's why she didn't make sense when she talked. She kept getting things mixed up and people mixed up. I guess she was mixed up. But he said it wasn't safe for her to be alone because she couldn't think properly. Anyway, that's what he said was the matter with her. And he said it keeps getting worse and that we had better do something before she had an accident of some kind."

"Then the doctor thought you were doing the right thing to find a safe place for your mother where she could be protected from falls or other accidents," the pastor said.

"Oh, yes. And my brother and sisters said the same. I called them all. You see they live all around the country. Chicago, Florida and Massachusetts. They all said the doctor was right and that I should go ahead and do whatever he thought best. You see, I am the one who has always lived near mother and kept an eye on her. I suppose I shouldn't say this, but the others never seemed to care very much just so long as I was nearby. They were always willing to give money if it was needed. But it really isn't. Lord knows it costs an arm and a leg, but we can swing that all right. That's not the problem. But I was the one who had to do it, and I saw her and I still see her and that is what gets me." Mrs. Folsome seemed to be simmering down and was slowly bringing some things into sharper focus.

"Yes, and as you point out some of the changes have come about because of different life styles, different modes of living. As you pointed out, a generation or two ago older folks were taken into stable families with large dwellings. There were few alternatives, and that was the way things had been done for a long time past. Now homes are different. Apartments are small and condominiums are minimal. Do you know that at the turn of the century, in 1900, seven of every ten families lived on a farm or in a small town? Now seven out of ten live in urban areas. You are right. There have been some great changes, and we are all caught up in them. What do we do about them?" the pastor asked.

"Is it as much as that?" Mrs. Folsome mused. "Of course we were brought up in a country town. I guess lots of people were, from what they say. But it is hard to think of so much change in just a lifetime. My mother has seen a lot of changes, automobiles, planes, telephones, TV and radio and now trips to the moon. We had kerosene lamps when I was a girl, and I can remember when we got lights. My mother has sure seen some changes."

"And there have been great changes in the way older people have been cared for. Do you remember any nursing homes or homes for the aged when you were a girl, Mrs. Folsome?"

"No, I guess not—just the country poor farm, and nobody would send a relative there if he had any self-respect. There was an awful stigma connected with that. When we were kids we would never go near it, because we heard all kinds of terrible stories about it." Mrs. Folsome shuddered.

The pastor said: "I remember those days. I am old enough to have visited in county homes for the poor and aged. We have come a long way in our lifetime. There is no comparison between a country poorhouse and a well-managed home for the aged and infirm. Tell me something about the home where your mother is."

Mrs. Folsome seemed to brighten up a bit. "Actually the

place where mother is is quite nice. It was a beautiful old home with lawns and trees all around it. Mother has a room with another lady who seemed to be having the same trouble as mother. There are trained nurses on duty night and day and people to clean the rooms and serve the meals. Mother is bathed and gets her hair done regularly. She can watch her favorite programs on TV. You know some of the people on those programs get to be like members of the family. Everybody is kind to mother, and I am sure she is well cared for.''

The pastor asked, "Do you think the doctor made a mistake to recommend this care for your mother?''

"Oh, no, of course not. He was doing what he thought was best for her. And he suggested a very good place, and everything is working out very well as far as that is concerned.''

The pastor continued, "But you think you made a mistake in following the doctor's advice?''

"When you look at it that way, of course, I did the best thing —the only thing. But it is still a terrible thing to have to do it.''

"Yes, I know, Mrs. Folsome. It does seem like a difficult thing to do, and it can be painful. Let's examine that a bit. Why would it be painful to do what you knew was the right thing to do?''

"You remember, a while ago we were talking about the county poor farm. I guess I still have some of the old feelings about putting the old folks away. But this is really different, and Lord knows we are not taking any charity—it costs us plenty.''

"But there is something else, Mrs. Folsome, that I am sure you have thought about many times,'' the pastor continued. "When someone we love and have felt was important in our lives gets old and changes we fight against those changes. We would like to deny them. We don't want to admit to ourselves that these changes are happening or have happened.''

"Oh, have you only spoken the truth,'' Mrs. Folsome said. "I go into the nursing home and speak to my mother and sometimes she acts as if she doesn't know me. And that hurts. It makes you realize that she won't be around long. What will life be without my mother?''

"Some of the grief we feel comes when we lose someone, and some of it comes when we know we are going to lose someone.

We can see it coming, and that hurts. And we have to go through a lot of changes in our thinking and feeling. We see the mother who has always been strong and dependable as a weak and confused little old lady, and it is painful," said the pastor.

Mrs. Folsome almost interrupted in her eagerness to speak. "That is so true. I don't think I have ever gone through anything that caused me so much distress as this thing with my mother. When I look at it sensibly I know that I was doing the right thing. I guess what hurts the most was that my brother and sisters made me do it all alone. I needed someone to keep telling me it was all right."

"Yes, that would have made a difference, I am sure," the pastor interjected. "But looked at from the other side it was a privilege to be able to care for your mother, and if others were not near, you were fortunate that you could do for her in her old age as she had done for you as a child—care for her when she couldn't care for herself."

"Well, I certainly wanted to do what I could. But what puzzles me is why I feel so guilty about doing what I knew I should?" Mrs. Folsome asked.

"Guilt is a feeling we have when we look at some realities in terms of our hopes and ideals. We call it existential guilt. When you see your mother failing it is a painful reality and you want to escape it. If you blame yourself you may say it is your fault and really your mother isn't failing, becoming senile. But you know you cannot deceive yourself like that. So you suffer as you bring the reality into focus. Sometimes this distorts other things. When you came in you had some things distorted. Maybe now we can see your feelings more clearly. Your feelings are good feelings, for they reflect your love. But we also have to face the truth that comes with change. You can't be blamed because your mother is growing old and showing the effects of aging."

"When you put it that way," Mrs. Folsome reflected, "it does seem different. Really I shouldn't blame myself. But it is all right to feel sad. I guess the simple fact is that the mother I knew is gone already. She looks the same but she isn't the same. I have to fix that in my mind. She has already changed. And I can care for her now when she can't understand, just like she did when I was a baby and didn't understand."

When Mrs. Folsome got up to leave she thanked her pastor for making everything so clear for her. And he thanked her for coming and assured her that anytime she was feeling upset about her mother she should stop in again and they would talk things over.

It is quite clear that the process of counseling has not changed the basic circumstances concerning the mother, but some relief of stress was apparent with the daughter. The basic problem of the wiser care of the aged remains untouched. The people who have to live the problem of major demographic changes may remain the primary concern of the pastor in such circumstances.

Chapter 27

Counseling with Members of the Team

The counseling tasks within the parish may often be shared with other professional persons. Sometimes in the preoccupation with the problems of the counselee it is possible to forget that the other members of the team are frail humans with problems of their own.

Members of the medical profession are subject to a type of pressure and burdens of responsibility that can on occasion become almost intolerable. They too need a chance to share their burdens with someone who can understand their feelings and can be trusted to keep them within the bounds of strict confidence. The following pastoral encounter was with a physician whose needs were great and whose opportunity for sharing them with another were clearly restricted.

It was past midnight, and the pastor was at work at his desk in a wing of his dwelling that was used for counseling. There were a private drive and a private entrance so that persons could come and go with ease. The pastor thought he heard footsteps on the porch, but they seemed tentative and he was not sure there was someone there until he heard a timid knock on the door.

When the pastor responded to the knock he saw a local physician standing in the darkness eight or ten feet back from the door. "Why, Doc, come in," he said. "What are you doing out this time of night? Coming back from your last housecall?"

Dr. Brownell dragged himself into the study and slumped down in an easy chair. He stretched his arms and legs a bit as if he were trying to make himself comfortable. "You won't believe this, but I've been driving around the block for half an hour. Wanted to come in and didn't. Kind of hoped your light would go out, but then I decided you were waiting up for me, so here I am."

"I'm glad I didn't go to bed, then. I'm sure you wouldn't call on me at this time of night unless you had a good reason."

"Oh, I've got reason enough." The doctor sat for quite some time as if trying to decide where to go from there. Because he was usually a highly articulate man, the pastor felt it was wise to let him take his own time.

Finally he said: "I suppose you want to know why I'm here. That would be reasonable. Well, to put it simply, I'm scared to death."

The pastor thought of a dozen things he could say but didn't say any of them. He watched the doctor intently.

The doctor continued: "I bet you never thought you'd hear me say anything like that. The big competent surgeon. The head of the surgical staff. It doesn't sound right, but that's the way it is." He looked intently at a picture on the wall, and the pastor remained silent.

"You don't know what it's like to take a knife to another human being. Everybody wants the doctor to do this and do that, but nobody ever asks what it's doing to the man behind the knife." And again there was a period of silence.

"Tomorrow morning I scrub for a brain tumor. I guess I've done it a couple of hundred of times, counting the army. But I've lost my nerve. I don't trust my hand. Look at the way it shakes. I don't think I can go through with it. And brother, I'm plain scared."

None of the things the pastor thought of saying seemed valid or useful at this point, so he continued to listen.

"You know, I'm in a funny spot. There's no one on earth I can talk to about this. I'd scare my wife if I tried to talk to her. If I mentioned it to anyone else on the staff I'd be in deep trouble in thirty minutes. You don't know what a hospital's like. I'd be reported, for the good of the patient, of course. I'd be examined. I'd be shelved. From that moment on there would be a big question mark after my name. Everybody'd know it. I'd be as good as finished." Again he paused for a long time.

"You know I hate shrinks. They know it too. If I went to one of those boys I'd be in worse trouble. Everyone would know it. What's worse than a nutty surgeon? I've thought of that route, and it's not for me. So here I am. You're the last resort I have. So I come to you, and I'm not sure why. What good does it do to pour it all out on you? You can't work a miracle and put me together again," he seemed a bit less resigned and a bit more angry. This might be a good sign.

"Maybe not, but I know something about stress and what it does to people," the pastor said. "I think I can help you relieve some of the tension that has built up."

"How can you do that?" Dr. Brownell asked.

"Just what we're doing now. Talking it out. Getting it into words. Hearing yourself talk."

"Yes, I guess you're right. But that doesn't get close to the real problem."

"How do you mean?"

Dr. Brownell thought awhile. Then he said, "It's the burden of omnipotence. It's life and death. You're right there. When things go right people take it for granted. That's the way it's supposed to be. But when they go wrong you're a criminal, a murderer ... You ought to hear what we have to take sometimes ... Like this tomorrow ... Cutting into somebody's brain. One slip and they're never right again. Every time you see them you feel guilty. It's too much to put on a man."

"The burden of omnipotence . . . You don't want it."

"Who needs it? People always expecting you to play God. I want no part of it. But how can you get away from it?"

"The role the doctor plays in the life of people is quite important. How do you feel about being a physician now?"

"All I ever wanted to be was a doctor. It was my all-consuming interest from way back. And I always wanted to be the best. That's why I kept on taking more study in surgery. And I'm good. I know it. I can cut circles around most of those guys. That is, when I'm good I'm hard to beat. But when I'm bad, you know, like the little girl with the curl—I can't face it . . . I can't face it."

"Just what is it you have trouble facing?"

Dr. Brownell sat thinking. Then he said: "You know, when you put it like that I can't come up with an easy answer. I know my stuff. I am where I wanted to be. You know, they're bringing people in from miles around. Medical school classes come to watch some of my work. But something's missing. It used to be every time I pulled on the gloves I became Superman. Now it's a chore. I don't feel the same about it."

"You mean it's something inside of you?" the pastor asked.

Again Dr. Brownell thought awhile. "Yes, it's something inside of me. I just don't hack it anymore. I've had twenty good years. But I don't look forward to doing the same thing for the next fifteen or twenty. I think you have to be really up to do good surgery. I'm not up anymore. I'm scared I'll muff it. The more scared I get the more shaky I get. I don't have any right to lift a knife to a person when I'm like this."

"So you have confidence in your basic skill as a surgeon, but somehow you've lost confidence in yourself. Is that what you're saying?"

"That doesn't sound right. But maybe it's true. It's like I'm running out of steam. I've noticed it coming on. I fought it off and told myself it wasn't true. The old drive just isn't there. How can a person keep on at a job like this with no drive?" Dr. Brownell asked.

"So you've run out of a sense of purpose. You had it for years, and then it began to slip away. Now you are frightened by the loss of it. Is that it?"

"That's pretty close to it."

"Let's go back and look at the purpose or drive you had. What was it that motivated you before?"

Again the doctor sat thinking for quite a while. "It's two things. One was to help people and the other was to get to the top."

"So you've made it to the top. What's so wrong with that?" the pastor queried.

"I don't like the implication of that. I think I hear what you're saying. Are you saying that I'm not really interested in helping people? That as long as I was moving up and I could use them for my purpose I had a purpose? But when I got there the game was over? Is that what you are saying?"

"You said that. But it's worth thinking about."

Dr. Brownell sat quietly for awhile, the muscles of his jaw expanding and contracting. Then he said, "That makes me sound like a rat, doesn't it? My ambition was the only thing that counted."

"No, I wouldn't put it that way. Your ambition was a valid and useful thing in helping you refine your skills. But now you've arrived at the place where the drive of ambition no longer serves its original purpose. Now you have what it takes to do a useful job with people but you need a new sense of satisfaction, a new sense of purpose. Right?"

Dr. Brownell seemed more relaxed now, less tense. He was beginning to show some interest in thinking about ideas.

"How do you mean, a new sense of purpose?" he asked.

The pastor continued: "When you're young you set goals, and they furnish incentive you need sometimes for many years. But when you arrive at those goals it is impossible to use the outworn incentive. Then you have to set some new goals, some more mature goals. When people get to your age they have a form of second adolescence. They have to figure out some goals that are good enough for the rest of their lives. It could be that's where you are now."

Dr. Brownell settled back in his chair and thought in silence for quite a while. Then he said: "You know, I think you've got something there. I've felt dissatisfied with myself and my life for some time, but I never gave it much careful thought. It was always the next job, an increasing demand for my services. I was a slave to my profession. But how do I shift gears now? How do I find a new philosophy of life at forty-eight?"

"You're in the prime of life. I can't think of a better time to have the adventure of finding a new and more adequate way of looking at yourself and life. You don't have to play games with yourself anymore. You can stand back and look at your life and decide what is a good enough meaning to attach your life to for the rest of your days."

"You make it sound interesting. But how do you go about reorganizing your life when it has been so structured for so long?" he asked.

"That's what religion is all about at its best. It is a matter of stimulating inner growth adequate to meet the needs of external circumstances. It tries to give answers to the questions of meaning. What is it all about? Now, here you are at forty-eight, with a significant skill and professional status. Are you the master of the skill and status or the slave of it? If you really want to help people, you have to start with yourself. You have to believe in yourself and in what you are doing."

"In other words you are telling me I need to grow up."

The pastor and the surgeon then spent an hour or more talking about concepts of inner growth and models of emotional and spiritual maturity. The distress that had been so obvious when Dr. Brownell came in seemed to have evaporated as this animated conversation went on. A number of interesting subjects were discussed, and it moved toward the idea of rededicating his skill as a gift of God and the service of humanity. The idea of a cosmic partnership which could use the best of him and give him the satisfaction of self-fulfillment seemed so important that Dr. Brownell suggested that there be a time of prayer and rededication. This was done, and he participated in a meaningful way.

It was three o'clock when the doctor looked at his watch and said with a startled expression: "I've got to be at the hospital at seven. That operation is scheduled for eight. And look at my hand. As steady as ever. You're right, it does help to unwind and talk about things. Thanks so much for everything."

As the doctor went out the door the pastor said, "Call me in the morning and tell me how the operation went."

On numerous occasions after that Dr. Brownell stopped in at the study to visit and talk. He said the prayer he had with the pastor had meant a lot and that now he made it a rule to go into a linen closet near the operating room for a time of prayer before each operation. That seemed to take care of the omnipotence problem, and he was never alone with his burdens, for his new partnership with a cosmic purpose gave him reassurance and purpose. And he often reported the new discoveries of wonder and beauty in life that developed as he sought to make his life the possessor of the skills and purposes rather than be the little man enslaved by the big skills.

So often the members of the caretaking team need each other just as much as others need them.

ANNOTATED BIBLIOGRAPHY

Persons who would explore further the literature on parish counseling will find much that is directly or indirectly useful. The personality sciences throw light on human behavior in ways that may be useful for the pastor who would understand his people. There is much of value that has not been mentioned in these pages. Only a small portion can be listed in this bibliography. What is mentioned can be the starting point for further exploration, for many of these books have extensive bibliographies of their own.

Some of the classics in pastoral care are still in print and should be in the basic library of every pastor.

Boisen, Anton. *Out of the Depths*. New York: Harper & Row, 1960; and *Explorations of the Inner World*. New York: Harper, 1936. A pioneer in clinical pastoral education, Boisen writes out of his own experience as a patient in a mental hospital. His sensitivity and concern have given a new dimension to the concept of pastoral care.
Cabot, Richard C. and Dicks, Russell L. *The Art of Ministering to the Sick*. New York: Macmillan, 1936. This classic in the pastoral care of the sick has been a training manual for years. It reflects the basis for cooperation between physician and pastor and gives new status to the function of pastoral care.
Cannon, Walter B. *The Wisdom of the Body*. New York: W. W. Norton, 1932. The relation of emotions to organic behavior both positively and negatively has created the context for pastoral care in recent years. This pioneering study opened up a new frontier.
Dunbar, Flanders. *Emotions and Bodily Changes*. New York: Columbia University Press, 1954. The next major step beyond Cannon, this is a comprehensive study of every aspect of organic behavior with an assessment of emotional roots. A basic reference work.

Hiltner, Seward. *Pastoral Counseling*. New York: Abingdon, 1949. In this book we have a basic statement concerning the nature and practice of pastoral counseling which has set the standard for most clinical training since its publication.

Jackson, Edgar N. *Understanding Grief*. New York: Abingdon, 1957. This book was the first full-length psychological study of this major emotion. It related pastoral care to an area of human vulnerability which has now become a basic concern for both medicine and the parish ministry.

Johnson, Paul E. *Psychology of Pastoral Care*. New York: Jason Aronson, 1975. Probably nothing better has been written as a comprehensive exploration of the many-faceted relationship of pastor and people.

It may be reassuring to the parish counselor to know that although clinical training is of recent origin, there is a long history and useful philosophy of pastoral care.

Clebsch, William A., and Jaekle, Charles. *Pastoral Care in Historical Perspective*. New York: Jason Aronson, 1975. Another perspective on pastoral care with scholarship and interpretation that will be useful to the pastor in assessing his role.

Hiltner, Seward. *Preface to Pastoral Theology*. New York: Abingdon, 1958. This book looks at the theological assumptions basic to the pastor's work with people. Many perspectives—biblical, historical, and practical—are utilized.

Jackson, Edgar N. *The Pastor and His People*. New York: Hawthorn, 1974. This exploration of relationships begins with a philosophical and theological examination of the meaning and validity of the pastoral role, primarily in counseling wtihin the parish.

Kelsey, Morton T. *Healing and Christianity*. New York: Harper & Row, 1973. Equally as scholarly as McNeill but from quite a different perspective. This work reflects the impact of psychosomatic research and is more contemporary. The author is a professor at Notre Dame in South Bend, Ind.

Kemp, Charles. *Physicians of the Soul*. New York: Macmillan, 1947. A readable and challenging look at the historical and contemporary resources for working with people.

McNeill, John T. *A History of the Cure of Souls*. New York: Harper, 1951. A scholarly treatment of the long interest in people and their welfare that has been a part of the history of pastoral care.

Several books must be mentioned as particularly useful in understanding the human personality and engaging in wise and useful counseling processes.

Farnsworth, Dana L., and Braceland, Francis J. *Psychiatry, The Clergy and Pastoral Counseling.* Collegeville, Minn.: Institute of Mental Health, St. John's University Press, 1969. A collection of papers that are designed to bring together the insights of psychiatry and the function of the parish ministry.

Horney, Karen. *Our Inner Conflicts.* New York: W. W. Norton, 1945. On these pages the pastor will find insight into the inner conflicts that disturb the neurotic personality along with some useful suggestions for therapy.

Levine, Maurice. *Psychotherapy in Medical Practice.* New York: Macmillan, 1949. Written for physicians, it is equally useful for a pastor. Economical in style and filled with practical insight, this book has an honored place in the literature of psychotherapy.

May, Rollo. *The Art of Counseling.* New York: Abingdon, 1939. Still a useful little book, this may be a good introduction to the various forms of movement that take place in counseling and the validity of the counselor's skills in observing, listening and evaluating.

Menninger, Karl. *The Human Mind.* New York: Knopf, 1945. Still one of the best sources of understanding the way mind and emotion work to produce behaviors. A basic work.

Rogers, Carl. *Counseling and Psychotherapy.* Boston: Houghton Mifflin, 1942. An essential book for understanding a method of counseling that has had a major impact on pastoral care. Should be read along with his more recent works on group processes.

Wise, Carroll A. *Pastoral Counseling: Its Theory and Practice.* New York: Harper, 1951. A pioneer in teaching pastoral care and counseling, Wise deals with the practical aspects as well as the theoretical disciplines that must be learned to be a good counselor.

The pastor's main tool in working with people is the skill with which he uses language in listening and in sharing his thoughts and feelings with others. So it is important for him to know as much as possible about this resource he uses. The following books illuminate the meaning and use of language.

Fast, Julius, *Body Language.* New York: Pocket Books, 1971. A small paperback with a readable approach to the meaning of facial expressions, gestures and unspoken forms of communication.

Jackson, Edgar N. *A Psychology for Preaching.* New York: Hawthorn, 1974. An effort to examine pulpit utterance to understand how it reflects the pastor's attitude toward people and affects their response toward him for any counseling relationship.

Ruesch, Jurgen, and Bateson, Gregory. *Communication*. New York: W. W. Norton, 1968; *Disturbed Communication*. New York: W. W. Norton, 1957; and *Therapeutic Communication*. New York: W. W. Norton, 1957. In these three books we find a comprehensive study of what language shows and how it can be used for healing. Basic works for the pastoral counselor.

Thass-Theinemann, Theodore. *The Interpretation of Language*. (2 vols.) New York: Jason Aronson, 1973. Here is an interpretation of the symbolic and unconscious uses of language as behavior that does for our verbal communication what Freud did for dreams.

A number of useful books focus on special situations and can be useful to the parish counselor in specialized areas of his work with people.

Bakan, David. *Disease, Pain and Sacrifice*. Chicago: University of Chicago Press, 1968. A study of contemporary insight on pain and suffering with an interesting interpretation of Job and the ancient ways of understanding and coping with pain.

Bowers, Margaretta, et al. *Counseling the Dying*. New York: Jason Aronson, 1975. A philosophical and practical look at the attitudes of professional workers with the dying, what the attitudes mean, and how they can be changed for the benefit of the patient.

Buber, Martin. *Between Man and Man*. New York: Macmillan, 1965. An Hassidic philosopher looks deeply into the nature and meaning of human relationships and discovers a common quest for the ultimate in human fulfillment through relationship and communication.

Fosdick, Harry E. *On Being a Real Person*. New York: Harper, 1943. An early effort to relate the parish ministry to the insights of psychology.

Frank, Jerome D. *Persuasion and Healing*. Baltimore: Johns Hopkins University Press, 1961. An exploration of medical and nonmedical factors involved in the healing process. Chapters on religion of special interest.

Frankl, Viktor E. *The Doctor and the Soul*. New York: Knopf, 1955. An examination of the moral or spiritual implications of the areas where the physician touches the inner being and must take some stands for the meaning of life and health. Points out the areas when pastor and physician meet in the healing process.

Jackson, Edgar N. *Coping with the Crises in Your Life*. New York: Hawthorn, 1974. The first effort to write a comprehensive basic text in crisis psychology and crisis management. Designed for the professional or nonprofessional who would understand how crises develop, how threatening they may be, and what can be done about their wise management.

LeShan, Eda. *The Wonderful Crisis of Middle Age.* New York: McKay, 1973. In a spritely style the author looks at the attitudes that may disrupt life in middle years and suggests wise adjustments that can lead to a fuller life.

Menninger, Karl. *Man Against Himself.* New York: Harcourt, Brace, 1938. Still a basic book in its useful exploration of aggressive behavior directed against the self.

Teilhard de Chardin, Pierre. *The Phenomenon of Man.* New York: Harper, 1959. An anthropologist with religious interests looks at man and his behavior and senses a move toward spiritual goals.

Warner, Lloyd. *The Family of God.* New Haven: Yale University Press, 1961. A sociologist examines group behavior and its meaning. Useful for the pastor in assessing community action.

Several journals also may be useful to pastors in improving their insight into human behavior and counseling skills.

The Bulletin of the Menninger Clinic, Topeka, Kansas
The Family Coordinator, 1219 University Ave., Minneapolis, Minn. 55414
Hastings Center Studies, Hastings-on-Hudson, N.Y. 10706
Humanistic Psychology, 416 Hoffman Ave., San Francisco, Calif. 94114
Journal of Marriage and the Family, 1219 University Ave., Minneapolis, Minn. 55414
Journal of Religion and Health, 16 E. 34th St., New York, N.Y. 10016
The Pastoral Counseling Review, 59 Fourth Ave., New York, N.Y. 10003

INDEX